HOUSE OF ABUNDANCE
PUBLICATIONS

Soaring Beyond the Horizon

Unveiling Extraordinary Airplane Facts and Discoveries

First edition

This book was professionally typeset on Reedsy.
Find out more at reedsy.com

To most people, the sky is the limit.
To those who love aviation, the sky is home.

Contents

1

Introduction

Since the Wright brothers' historic flight in 1903, airplanes have captured the imagination of people worldwide. The ability to soar through the skies, defy gravity, and travel to distant lands has always been a dream of humanity. From the early pioneers of aviation to the modern marvels of engineering, airplanes have continuously evolved, shaping history and revolutionizing how we connect with the world.

Welcome to "Soaring Beyond the Horizon: Unveiling Extraordinary Airplane Facts and Discoveries." In this captivating journey, we will embark on an exploration of the remarkable world of aviation. This book aims to take you on a thrilling ride through the annals of aviation history, the wonders of aircraft technology, and the groundbreaking discoveries that have propelled humanity to new heights.

Throughout the chapters, we will delve into the intricacies of airplane design and the principles of flight. We will uncover the secrets behind aerodynamics, thrust, and lift, demystifying the forces that enable airplanes to defy gravity and cruise through the air. From the early propeller-driven aircraft to cutting-edge jet engines and beyond, we will witness the remarkable evolution of aviation technology.

But this journey is not just about the mechanics of flight. It is about the impact of airplanes on our society, economy, and culture. We will explore how aviation has transformed the way we travel, trade, and connect with one another across continents and oceans. From the pioneers who pushed the boundaries of human achievement to the modern-day adventurers exploring the frontiers of space, we will meet the visionaries who shaped the course of aviation history.

As we turn each page, we will uncover fascinating airplane facts and discoveries that will leave you in awe of the incredible achievements of human ingenuity. We will soar with the daring aviators who broke records and barriers and celebrate the triumphs of engineering that made the impossible possible.

"Soaring Beyond the Horizon" is not just a book but a celebration of the indomitable human spirit and our relentless pursuit of the skies. So fasten your seatbelts, stow your tray tables, and prepare for an exhilarating flight into the world of aviation, where dreams take flight and the sky is never the limit.

2

The Marvelous Airframe

Definition and Significance of the Airframe

I n the vast world of aviation, the airframe is the backbone of every aircraft, encompassing its structural integrity and shaping its aerodynamic capabilities. The following chapter takes us on a captivating exploration of the marvel that is the airframe, revealing its fundamental definition and unparalleled significance in the realm of flight.

The airframe is more than just a mere framework; it is the essence of an aircraft's existence. We delve into the intricate details of its construction, from the early days of wooden frames with fabric wings to the revolutionary all-metal designs that shaped the course of aviation history. Through the lens of history, we witness how the progression of technology paved the way for the development of lightweight and robust structures that now grace our skies.

As we venture deeper into the heart of the airframe, we uncover the secret behind the lift that keeps airplanes airborne. A closer look at airfoil cross-sections and wing designs reveals the ingenuity behind generating the lifting force that defies gravity. We explore how wings transform air pressure into lift, allowing an aircraft to defy gravity and soar above the horizon.

The airframe's configuration also plays a pivotal role in an aircraft's stability and performance. Discover the captivating variations in wing plans, from monoplanes and biplanes to the innovative designs of the flying wing and blended wing body. We unravel the engineering behind each configuration, delving into the trade-offs and advantages they offer in different flight regimes.

Beyond its engineering prowess, the airframe is a testament to human innovation and determination. The stories of aviation pioneers who pushed the boundaries of what was possible inspire us to appreciate the audacity of dreamers who dared to challenge the status quo.

Evolution of Airplane Materials: From Wood to Composite Materials

In the early 20th century, wooden structures formed the backbone of aviation, with skilled artisans meticulously fashioning wooden frames to support fabric wings. Despite limited resources and technology, these pioneering aircraft showcased the ingenuity and determination of aviators to conquer the skies.

The advent of metal mounts ushered in a new era of strength and durability in aviation. The transition from wood to metal airframes marked a pivotal moment in aircraft construction history, providing a foundation for robust planes capable of withstanding higher speeds and altitudes.

As aviation demands progressed, the quest for lighter yet stronger materials advanced parallel. A significant breakthrough occurred with the emergence of aluminum alloys, revolutionizing the industry and introducing a new era of faster and more efficient aircraft. We trace how aluminum alloys swiftly became the material of choice for countless airplanes, proving their mettle in military and commercial aviation.

This exploration extends to the rise of composite materials, which came about from pursuing even more outstanding performance and efficiency. The revolutionary era of carbon fiber composites is unveiled, showcasing the fusion of solid fibers and lightweight resins that opened new frontiers in aircraft design. From the Boeing 787 Dreamliner to the Airbus A350 XWB, we witness the breathtaking achievements of planes crafted from these cutting-edge materials.

Beyond carbon fiber, our exploration encompasses other composite materials such as fiberglass, Kevlar, and titanium composites, each bringing unique strengths to the aviation landscape. These materials have broken the traditional constraints of aircraft design, enabling engineers to craft sleeker, fuel-efficient, and environmentally friendly planes.

This testament to the ever-evolving nature of aviation materials, innovation, and creativity propels us beyond the boundaries of what was once thought possible. As we trace the evolution from wood to composite materials, we gain a profound appreciation for the pivotal role of materials in shaping the extraordinary airplanes that grace our skies today.

Key Components of the Airframe: Wings, Fuselage, Vertical Stabilizer, Horizontal Stabilizer, and Landing Gear

Now, we direct our attention to the vital components that constitute the extraordinary airframe, serving as the very backbone of each aircraft. Every element is critical in ensuring the plane's stability, control, and safety, culminating in the awe-inspiring flight experience we relish today.

Wings: The Defiant Lift Generators

The essence of flight lies within the heart of a plane's wings, their far-reaching grasp on air not just a static presence but a powerful dynamic dance. Their complex shapes, more specifically the curvature of the airfoil, form an intricate framework that yields the invaluable force we know as lift. With every flex and arch, they orchestrate the masterful symphony of defying gravity, keeping us suspended above the horizon.

Indeed, a captivating journey through time reflects the evolution of wings, from the humble roots of early biplanes to the technological marvels seen in contemporary airliners and formidable fighter jets. Every bend, every angle, and every notch in these structures contain a riveting narrative of human ingenuity and our enduring quest to master the skies. The canvas of wings, colored by science and aerodynamics, is not just a tale of mechanical prowess but a testament to the enchanting allure of flight.

Fuselage: The Aerodynamic Envelope

The fuselage, the sleek, streamlined body of an aircraft, not only houses the flight crew, passengers, and cargo but also cradles the plane's crucial systems. It's a closer inspection of this part of an airplane that allows us to trace the intriguing progression of its design. We see it evolve from a mere wooden skeleton in the early days of aviation to the modern era's seamless constructions of metal and composite materials.

The engineers' art of balancing act truly brings the fuselage to life. They finely calibrate the scale between sturdiness and weight, ensuring the fuselage withstands the rigors of flight while promoting maximum fuel efficiency. This complex dance of power and performance encapsulates the innovative spirit of aviation engineering, a testament to our unending quest for improved flight.

Vertical Stabilizer: The Silent Guardian of Yaw

The vertical stabilizer, positioned at the tail end of an aircraft, is integral to maintaining flight stability by counteracting the aircraft's yawing motion - a sideways movement around its vertical axis - the vertical stabilizer enables smooth, controlled directional changes. This component varies in design and size to suit each aircraft type. Its evolution from fundamental to sophisticated forms mirrors advancements in aviation engineering, particularly in material use and aerodynamics.

Although not always visible, the vertical stabilizer is a crucial flight element, tirelessly ensuring smooth and secure travel. Its role is a testament to human ingenuity in mastering the complexities of flight.

Horizontal Stabilizer: Controlling the Pitch

The horizontal stabilizer, nestled near the aircraft's tail, controls the plane's pitch and the motion around its lateral axis. It adjusts the aircraft's nose-up or nose-down attitudes, influencing ascent, descent, and maintaining altitude. Key to this control are the elevators and sophisticated fly-by-wire systems. These precisely adjust the stabilizer's angle, converting pilot inputs into specific stabilizer movements. The horizontal stabilizer's evolution reflects progress in aviation technology. Initially rudimentary, it has become highly sophisticated, enhancing flight safety and efficiency. Although less visible, the horizontal stabilizer is crucial in every flight, embodying human innovation in aviation.

Landing Gear: Graceful Touchdowns

The landing gear, a vital component of an aircraft, facilitates smooth takeoffs, landings, and ground movements. It is designed to withstand the plane's weight and ensures stationary balance. Landing gear can vary from wheels to floats or skis and is configured according to the aircraft's design and function. Configurations range from the basic taildragger in older planes to the tricycle setup in modern aircraft or the complex assemblies on large airliners. The landing gear houses several intricate systems, including shock absorbers, retracting mechanisms for flight efficiency, and braking systems for ground control. Despite its evolution with aviation advancements, the landing gear often operates behind the scenes. Yet, its role in connecting sky and earth journeys is indispensable, underscoring the beauty of aviation engineering.

Advantages and Disadvantages of Different Airframe Configurations

Airframe configurations are crucial in determining an aircraft's performance, stability, and overall capabilities. In this section, we delve into the various airframe designs and examine their unique advantages and disadvantages.

Monoplane

Defined by a single main wing, monoplanes enjoy the advantages of a straightforward, streamlined design. This reduces drag and boosts speed while facilitating efficient lift generation suited to high-speed flight. Moreover, easier maintenance and component accessibility come as added benefits. However, monoplanes face challenges, including a limited wing area that may result in lower lift capacity and diminished stability, particularly at low speeds.

Biplane

Biplanes, which sport two stacked wings, boast an increased wing area that offers more lift and superior maneuverability. This configuration also provides enhanced structural strength, supporting a higher load-carrying capacity and improved stability during slow flight and takeoff. Yet, the additional wing results in higher drag and a more complex design, leading to increased manufacturing and maintenance expenses.

Canard

Distinguished by a small forewing situated ahead of the main wing, canards offer improved stall resistance and amplified low-speed maneuverability. They also provided superior control authority for responsiveness and reduced aerodynamic stalls and spin risks. However, canards can increase the complexity of control systems and cause aerodynamic interference between the canard and the main wing.

Flying Wing

Comprising a wing and nothing else, flying wings promise reduced drag and improved fuel efficiency due to the absence of a fuselage. They also present enhanced stealth capabilities with a reduced radar cross-section and the potential for increased payload capacity. Despite these advantages, flying wings are challenging to stabilize and control without a traditional tail and offer limited space for crew, passengers, and equipment.

Tandem Wing

Featuring two wings placed one behind the other, tandem wings deliver increased lift and stability. They also ensure enhanced maneuverability and control at different speeds and offer the potential for unconventional payload arrangements. However, they also introduce increased structural complexity, weight, and higher aerodynamic drag, which can impact overall performance.

Understanding the trade-offs between these airframe configurations is essential for aircraft designers and engineers. Each design serves specific purposes and excels in certain flight conditions. By exploring the advantages and disadvantages of these airframe types, we gain valuable insights into the evolution of aviation design and the ingenuity of aerospace pioneers. As we continue our exploration, we'll discover how these configurations have shaped the remarkable airplanes that have soared beyond the horizon of conventional flight.

Historical Examples of Famous Airplanes with Unique Airframe Designs

Throughout the history of aviation, visionary engineers and daring pilots have pushed the boundaries of airframe design, creating iconic aircraft with unconventional configurations. This section uncovers some historical examples of famous airplanes that stand out for their remarkable and innovative airframe designs.

The Horten Ho 229

The Horten Ho 229, also known as the "Flying Wing," was a revolutionary jet-powered aircraft developed by the Horten brothers, Walter and Reimar, during World War II. Its distinctive flying wing design eliminated the need for a conventional fuselage and tail, reducing drag and radar visibility. The Ho 229 was intended to be a stealthy, high-speed reconnaissance and bomber aircraft. Still, its development was cut short due to the war's end. Nevertheless, it laid the groundwork for future flying wing concepts, inspiring modern stealth aircraft like the Northrop B-2 Spirit.

The Boulton Paul Defiant

The Boulton Paul Defiant was a unique turret fighter aircraft the Royal Air Force used during World War II. Unlike traditional fighters, the Defiant featured a "turret" in the rear cockpit armed with machine guns. This unconventional design was intended to provide increased firepower and defensive capabilities. However, it proved vulnerable to attacks from the rear, leading to its eventual reassignment as a night fighter and target-towing aircraft.

The Grumman X-29

The Grumman X-29 was an experimental aircraft developed in the 1980s to explore advanced aerodynamics and control systems. Its forward-swept wing design was a departure from conventional aircraft configurations. The X-29 aimed to test the advantages and challenges of forward-swept wings, such as improved agility and maneuverability at high angles of attack. Although the X-29 demonstrated some promising results, its complex design and control issues limited its potential for production aircraft.

The Vought V-173 "Flying Pancake"

The Vought V-173, nicknamed the "Flying Pancake," was an

experimental aircraft designed during World War II. Its unique circular airframe resembled a pancake and was intended to maximize lift efficiency. The V-173 utilized contra-rotating propellers and a unique "all-wing" design, allowing it to take off and land slowly. While it never entered full-scale production, the V-173's unconventional design contributed valuable insights to future VTOL (Vertical Takeoff and Landing) aircraft development.

The Rutan VariEze

The Rutan VariEze was a homebuilt aircraft designed by Burt Rutan in the 1970s. Its canard configuration with a forward wing and rear-mounted pusher propeller differed from traditional aircraft designs. The VariEze showcased the feasibility of efficient canard designs for general aviation aircraft, offering improved stall resistance and maneuverability. The success of the VariEze influenced the design of Rutan's later aircraft, including the famous Rutan Voyager, which circumnavigated the globe without refueling.

These historical examples highlight the adventurous spirit of aviation pioneers who dared to challenge conventional thinking and push the limits of airframe design. Their innovations paved the way for the incredible diversity of aircraft we see today, each with its unique configuration tailored to meet specific mission requirements. As we continue our journey through aviation, we'll encounter even more extraordinary airplanes that have left an indelible mark on the skies above.

3

Exploring Wing Configurations

Understanding the Role of Wings in Lift Generation

Wings are one of the most critical components of an aircraft, responsible for generating the lift force necessary to keep the airplane airborne. This chapter explores the fascinating world of wing configurations and reviews the principles behind lift generation.

The Airfoil Shape

At the heart of every wing lies the airfoil shape, pivotal in creating lift. An airfoil is designed with a curved upper surface and a flatter lower surface, resulting in differences in air pressure above and below the wing. As the aircraft moves forward, air flows over the wings, with the faster-moving air above the wing creating lower pressure than the slower-moving air below. This pressure difference produces an upward force, lifting the aircraft off the ground.

Aspect Ratio and Wing Span

The aspect ratio of a wing is the ratio of its span to its chord (width). High aspect ratio wings, with longer spans and narrower chords, offer higher lift efficiency, generating less induced drag. Conversely, low aspect ratio wings provide better maneuverability and are commonly found in fighter jets and aerobatic aircraft.

Swept Wings

Sweeping the wings backward or forward can significantly impact an aircraft's performance, especially at transonic speeds. Swept wings help delay the onset of shock waves and reduce drag, making them beneficial for high-speed flight. These wing configurations are commonly used in supersonic aircraft and commercial airliners.

Delta Wings

Delta wings, characterized by their triangle-like shape, have unique advantages in specific flight regimes. They offer excellent high-speed performance and high lift-to-drag ratios, making them suitable for supersonic flight. Delta wings are commonly found in advanced fighter jets and high-speed research aircraft.

Variable Geometry Wings

Specific aircraft have variable geometry wings that can change their shape during flight. These wings allow aircraft to optimize their performance for different flight conditions. By adjusting the wing's sweep angle or span, variable geometry wings offer enhanced flexibility and efficiency across a wide range of speeds.

Blended Wing Bodies

Blended wing bodies represent a fusion of the fuselage and wing, offering a unique and aerodynamically efficient design. These aircraft feature flattened and airfoil-shaped bodies contributing to lift generation, reducing the need for traditional wings. Blended wing bodies show promise in increasing fuel efficiency and payload capacity for future commercial aircraft.

As we explore the myriad wing configurations, we uncover the art and science behind lift generation, making it possible for airplanes to conquer the skies. Each wing design represents a delicate balance between aerodynamic performance, structural integrity, and the aircraft's intended mission. Join us as we soar further into aviation to uncover more captivating discoveries that make flight possible.

Monoplanes vs. Biplanes: A Historical Comparison

In the early days of aviation, aircraft designers experimented with various wing configurations to find the most efficient and stable design. Two prominent wing structures emerged as contenders for dominance: monoplanes and biplanes. In this section, we embark on a historical journey to compare and contrast the development and impact of monoplanes and biplanes on aviation.

Monoplanes: Embracing Simplicity and Speed

Monoplanes, characterized by their single-wing design, gained popularity as aviation technology advanced. They offered several advantages over biplanes, including:

- **Streamlined Design**: Monoplanes boasted a sleek and streamlined appearance, reducing drag and increasing overall speed. This design allowed them to achieve higher speeds than their biplane counterparts.
- **Structural Efficiency**: Monoplanes require fewer structural components than biplanes, making them lighter and more maneuverable. The absence of interplane struts and wires simplified construction and maintenance.
- **Higher Altitude Performance:** Monoplanes proved more adept at flying at higher altitudes due to their better aerodynamic efficiency. This advantage made them suitable for long-distance flights and military reconnaissance missions.

Notable Monoplanes

- **The Spirit of St. Louis**: Charles Lindbergh's legendary monoplane, which made the first non-stop transatlantic flight in 1927, captured the world's imagination and revolutionized long-distance air travel.
- **Messerschmitt Bf 109**: World War II's iconic German fighter plane, renowned for its agility and deadly effectiveness in aerial combat.

Biplanes: Versatility and Agility in the Skies

Biplanes, featuring two wings stacked one above the other, were initially favored for their stability and agility. Their unique characteristics included:

- **Enhanced Lift**: Biplanes generated more lift due to the additional wing, making them ideal for early aircraft that lacked powerful engines. This allowed for shorter takeoff and landing distances.
- **Maneuverability**: The staggered wing design of biplanes provided superior control and maneuverability, making them popular choices for aerobatic displays and dogfights during World War I.
- **Robust Structure**: Biplanes were inherently stronger and could withstand higher loads, making them suitable for military applications and rugged terrains.

Notable Biplanes

- **Boeing Stearman**: A classic biplane used extensively as a military trainer during World War II and renowned for its stable flight characteristics.
- **Sopwith Camel**: One of the most iconic biplanes of World War I, known for its lethal dogfighting capabilities and distinctive humped cowling.

The Evolution of Wing Configurations

As aviation technology progressed, monoplanes eventually surpassed biplanes in popularity due to their higher speeds and greater operational range. However, biplanes continued to serve specialized roles, such as crop dusting, aerial firefighting, and aerobatic displays. Their robust structure and agility still make them valuable assets in specific applications.

The Benefits of Swept Wings and Their Impact on Supersonic Flight

As aviation technology advanced, engineers and designers began exploring innovative ways to improve aircraft performance, particularly at higher speeds and during supersonic flight. One crucial breakthrough that revolutionized aerodynamics was the introduction of swept wings. In this section, we unravel the benefits of swept wings and their significant impact on supersonic flight.

Understanding the Concept of Swept Wings

Swept wings refer to a wing configuration where the wing's leading edge is swept backward, forming an angle with the aircraft's longitudinal axis. This design differs from traditional straight wings and offers several key advantages, particularly in high-speed flight.

Supersonic Flight Challenges

During the early days of supersonic flight experimentation, aircraft encountered numerous challenges as they approached the speed of sound. At transonic speeds (close to the speed of sound), shock waves and drag increase, causing turbulence and stability issues. These aerodynamic challenges posed severe limitations on aircraft performance and safety.

Benefits of Swept Wings

Sweeping the wings backward solved the challenges faced in supersonic flight. The benefits of swept wings include:

- **Delaying Drag Rise**: Swept wings effectively delayed the on-set of shock waves and drag rise as the aircraft approached the speed of sound. This reduced drag and turbulence, allowing aircraft to achieve higher speeds without encountering critical aerodynamic issues.
- **Improved Stability**: The swept wing design improved lateral stability and made aircraft more controllable at high speeds. It enhanced the aircraft's ability to recover from rolls and provided smoother handling during supersonic flight.
- **Reducing Wave Drag**: As aircraft surpassed the speed of sound, they encountered a new type of drag called wave drag. Swept wings helped mitigate wave drag by dispersing the shock waves generated at supersonic speeds along the wing's surface, minimizing the impact of this additional drag force.

Historical Impact

Swept wings played a pivotal role in the development of super-sonic aircraft, enabling the successful design and operation of several famous planes, including:

- **North American X-15**: A rocket-powered aircraft used for experimental research and space exploration, achieving speeds of Mach 6.7 and altitudes beyond the Earth's atmosphere.

· **Concorde**: A supersonic passenger airliner capable of flying at Mach 2.04 and connecting distant destinations in record time.

Continuing Innovations

Over the years, aerospace engineers continued to refine the design of swept wings, leading to advanced variations such as variable-sweep wings. These innovations allowed aircraft to adapt their wing configuration in-flight, optimizing performance at different speeds and altitudes.

Delta Wings and Their Application in High-Speed and Maneuverable Aircraft

The quest for even greater speed and maneuverability in aircraft led to the development of another groundbreaking wing configuration known as the delta wing. In this section, we explore delta wings and their application in high-speed and agile aircraft.

Understanding Delta Wings

Delta wings are a distinctive triangular-shaped wing configuration with the leading edge forming a sharp angle resembling the Greek letter "delta." This unique design differs significantly from conventional swept and straight wings, offering distinct advantages for specific flight regimes.

High-Speed Performance

Delta wings are particularly well-suited for high-speed flight, especially in the transonic and supersonic regions. Their sharp leading edge helps delay the onset of shock waves, reducing drag and improving aerodynamic efficiency at high velocities.

Maneuverability

The delta wing's distinctive shape provides exceptional maneuverability, making it an ideal choice for agile fighter aircraft. The wing's large surface area and high aspect ratio allow superior roll rates and quick response to pilot inputs, enabling precise aerial maneuvers and dogfighting capabilities.

Supersonic Stability

Delta wings also contribute to enhanced supersonic stability. Their low wing loading and unique aerodynamic characteristics minimize pitch-up effects and provide a more stable platform during high-speed flight, ensuring better control and handling.

Leading Examples

Several famous aircraft have employed delta wings to achieve remarkable performance:

· Convair F-102 Delta Dagger: The F-102 was the world's first operational delta-wing supersonic interceptor. It was vital to the United States Air Force's air defense during the Cold

War.

- Dassault Mirage III: The Mirage III, a French-built delta-wing fighter, gained fame for its exceptional speed and versatility, becoming one of the most successful aircraft.
- Eurofighter Typhoon: A modern multirole fighter, the Typhoon's delta wing design contributes to its outstanding agility, allowing it to excel in air-to-air and air-to-ground missions.

Challenges and Considerations

While delta wings offer numerous advantages, they present some challenges, particularly in subsonic flight. Their high lift-to-drag ratio at supersonic speeds may increase drag during subsonic flight, impacting fuel efficiency.

Advanced Variations

Aerospace engineers have continued to innovate with delta wing configurations, developing various modifications and combinations, such as the canard-delta configuration. These variations optimize performance across different flight regimes, combining the advantages of both delta and canard wings.

Blended Wing Body: The Future of Fuel-Efficient Airplane Design

In recent years, aerospace engineers have been exploring revolutionary designs to enhance the efficiency and sustainability of aircraft. Among these innovative concepts, the blended wing body (BWB) has emerged as a promising breakthrough in aviation engineering. In this section, we sift through the composite wing body concept and uncover its potential as the future of fuel-efficient airplane design.

Definition and Characteristics

The blended wing body is a radical departure from the traditional tube-and-wing configuration of most commercial airplanes. It combines the wing and fuselage into a seamless, smoothly blended structure, resulting in a vast, flattened body that resembles a flying wing. This unique shape offers several distinct advantages over conventional designs.

Fuel Efficiency Advantages

The primary motivation behind the blended wing body design is to achieve remarkable fuel efficiency. By eliminating the fuselage and wing junction, the BWB reduces aerodynamic drag, reducing fuel consumption during flight. The aircraft's expansive wing surfaces enhance lift-to-drag ratios, improving fuel efficiency.

Increased Passenger Capacity

The blended wing body's wide and spacious interior provides ample cabin space, enabling it to accommodate significantly more passengers and cargo than traditional aircraft. This increased capacity holds the potential to revolutionize commercial air travel by offering greater seating availability and cargo capabilities.

Enhanced Environmental Performance

As the aviation industry strives to reduce environmental impact, the blended wing body's fuel efficiency aligns with its sustainability goals. Its reduced fuel consumption results in lower greenhouse gas emissions and a smaller carbon footprint, making it an attractive option for eco-conscious airlines and regulators.

Improved Noise Reduction

The seamless integration of the wing and body in the BWB design also reduces flight noise. The absence of wing-fuselage joints and airflow redistribution contribute to quieter operations, benefiting passengers and communities around airports.

Challenges and Advancements

Despite its many advantages, the blended wing body design presents engineering challenges. Ensuring structural integrity, proper weight distribution, and stability require innovative engineering solutions. Researchers and aerospace companies continually advance their understanding of these challenges to make BWB designs viable for commercial use.

Promising Prototypes

Several research institutions and aerospace companies have developed functional blended wing body prototypes, showcasing the design's potential. These experimental aircraft are crucial steps toward realizing the full potential of the BWB concept in commercial aviation.

Future of Flight

The blended wing body design holds tremendous promise as the aviation industry looks toward a more sustainable future. Its fuel efficiency, increased capacity, and environmental advantages position it as a leading contender for the next generation of commercial aircraft.

4

Mastering Flight Controls and Instruments

Importance of Flight Controls in Maneuvering the Aircraft

Mastering flight controls is a fundamental aspect of piloting an aircraft in aviation. This chapter goes deep into the crucial role flight controls play in maneuvering and maintaining control of an airplane throughout its flight. From the earliest days of aviation to the cutting-edge technology used in modern aircraft, flight controls have remained an indispensable element in the art and science of flying.

The Primary Flight Controls

The chapter begins by exploring the primary flight controls: ailerons, elevators, and rudder. Each control serves a specific purpose in maneuvering the aircraft around its three axes: roll, pitch, and yaw. We delve into the principles behind these control surfaces and how pilots use them to precisely navigate the skies.

Fly-by-Wire Technology

The advent of fly-by-wire technology marked a significant turning point in aircraft control systems. This innovation replaced conventional mechanical linkages with electronic interfaces, thus catapulting the domain of aviation into an era of increased precision and responsiveness. Fly-by-wire systems enhance safety by offering more accurate control during standard flight conditions and substantially reducing the risk of incidents such as stalls or loss of control. These systems integrate cutting-edge technology with complex aerodynamics to streamline aircraft operations, encapsulating the commitment of the aviation industry to constantly improve and evolve in the face of technological advancements for optimal safety outcomes.

Control Sensitivity and Feedback

Control sensitivity and feedback are fundamental elements in aircraft operation, allowing pilots to maintain precise command over their planes. Sensitivity relates to the degree of response from the aircraft to the pilot's control inputs. At the same time, feedback is the tactile response a pilot feels, providing crucial information about how the aircraft reacts. Achieving the right balance between these two aspects is vital, as it influences the pilot's ability to respond to different flight conditions effectively. This can range from the fine control needed during takeoff and landing to the more subtle adjustments during high-altitude cruising. The nuances of control sensitivity and feedback, thus, constitute an essential part of the art and science of flying.

Secondary and Tertiary Controls

Beyond the primary flight controls, we uncover the role of secondary and tertiary controls, such as flaps, slats, spoilers, and trim tabs. These additional mechanisms fine-tune the aircraft's performance and allow pilots to optimize various aspects of the flight.

The Cockpit: Instruments and Displays

The cockpit, often termed the aircraft's command center, is brimming with various instruments and displays that assist pilots in operating the aircraft effectively and safely. These tools provide vital information about the plane's status and its environment. Devices such as altimeters, airspeed, and attitude indicators inform pilots about the aircraft's altitude, speed, and orientation. Navigation displays, meanwhile, guide the pilots along their planned route, ensuring they reach their destination accurately and efficiently. Comprehending the function of each instrument and displaying it in the cockpit is integral to mastering flight control and decision-making in aviation.

Autopilot Systems

Autopilot systems have become integral to modern aviation, particularly in commercial flights. These advanced systems, designed to automatically control the trajectory of an aircraft, play a crucial role in maintaining stable flight and adjusting the aircraft's heading, altitude, and speed without continuous input from the pilots. Particularly useful during long-haul flights, autopilots help to alleviate the pilot's workload, allowing them to focus more on monitoring the aircraft's overall status and managing unforeseen circumstances. The continuing advancements in autopilot technology signal a promising future for safer, more efficient, and increasingly automated air travel.

Redundancy and Safety

In aviation, redundancy is a fundamental principle designed to enhance safety. It refers to the provision of multiple independent systems performing the same function. So, in a failure in one system, others can take over, ensuring uninterrupted operation. Critical systems such as engines, avionics, hydraulic, and flight control systems often have built-in redundancies. The concept also extends to pilot training, where pilots are trained to handle various emergency scenarios. Although complex and costly, this high level of redundancy underscores the industry's commitment to safety, emphasizing the goal of making every flight a safe journey.

Human-Machine Interaction

The interplay between pilots and flight control systems is vital to aviation safety. This relationship is anchored in human factors and cockpit ergonomics, which study the most efficient and safe ways pilots interact with their machines. Successful human-machine interaction promotes effective communication and cooperation between pilots and automated systems. This optimizes the aircraft's performance and significantly bolsters overall flight safety. By understanding and addressing these interactions, we can design more intuitive and responsive systems that support pilots in making critical decisions and managing the complex tasks involved in flying an aircraft.

Detailed Explanation of Ailerons, Elevators, and Rudder Functions

This section looks at the essential flight controls known as ailerons, elevators, and rudder, which form the primary means of maneuvering an aircraft. Understanding the functions of these control surfaces is crucial for pilots to achieve stable and controlled flight in various flight conditions.

Ailerons

Ailerons are hinged control surfaces mounted on the trailing edge of an aircraft's wings, one on each wing. Their primary function is to control the aircraft's roll around its longitudinal axis. When a pilot operates the control column or yoke, the ailerons move in opposite directions—one goes up while the other goes down. This movement creates differential lift on each wing, causing the aircraft to roll either left or right. By altering the lift on each wing, ailerons allow the pilot to bank the plane, initiate turns, and maintain balance during maneuvers. Ailerons are crucial for coordinated turns and lateral stability in flight.

Elevators

Elevators are horizontal control surfaces positioned on the trailing edge of the aircraft's horizontal stabilizer, typically at the rear of the fuselage. They are responsible for controlling the aircraft's pitch around its lateral axis. When the pilot pulls back on the control column or yoke, the elevators deflect upward, increasing the lift on the tail and causing the nose of the aircraft to pitch up. Conversely, pushing the control column forward deflects the elevators downward, reducing lift on the tail and causing the nose to pitch down. Elevators are essential for controlling the aircraft's attitude during climbs, descents, and level flight.

Rudder

The rudder is a vertical control surface attached to the trailing edge of the aircraft's vertical stabilizer, usually located at the rear of the fuselage. Its primary function is to control the aircraft's yaw around its vertical axis. The rudder deflects left or right when the pilot applies rudder input using the rudder pedals. This action creates varying amounts of drag on one side of the aircraft's tail, initiating a yawing motion. The rudder is instrumental in maintaining coordinated flight during turns, crosswind landings, and controlling the aircraft's heading.

Balancing and Coordinating Controls

Effective piloting involves a coordinated use of ailerons, elevators, and rudders to maneuver the aircraft smoothly and efficiently. Coordinated flight means using these control surfaces to minimize adverse effects such as yaw, which can cause uncoordinated turns and a slip or skid. Adverse yaw occurs because ailerons create more drag on the descending wing during a turn. Pilots ensure the aircraft maintains a coordinated and stable flight path by using the rudder in conjunction with ailerons.

The proper use of ailerons, elevators, and rudder allows pilots to navigate the skies confidently, performing turns, climbs, and descents with precision. This seamless coordination of primary flight controls is the essence of mastering flight. It is essential for pilots to safely and skillfully operate aircraft of all types and sizes.

The Role of the Throttle in Controlling Engine Power and Speed

In this section, we discuss the critical role of the throttle in controlling an aircraft's engine power and speed. The throttle is a primary control that allows pilots to regulate the fuel-air mixture delivered to the engine, influencing its power output and, consequently, the aircraft's performance.

The Function of the Throttle

The throttle is typically located in the aircraft's cockpit, within reach of the pilot's hand or fingers. It is connected to the engine's fuel system and controls fuel flow to its combustion chambers. By adjusting the throttle, the pilot can increase or decrease the engine's power output, directly affecting the aircraft's speed, rate of climb, and overall performance.

Increasing Engine Power

When a pilot pushes the throttle forward, more fuel is introduced into the engine's cylinders. As a result, the engine generates greater power, leading to increased thrust produced by the propeller or jet engines. This increased thrust allows the aircraft to accelerate, climb steeply, or overcome aerodynamic drag during takeoff or in adverse weather conditions.

Decreasing Engine Power

Conversely, pulling the throttle back reduces the fuel flowing to the engine, resulting in decreased power output. Lower engine power reduces the thrust generated by the propulsion system, leading to a decrease in the aircraft's speed and rate of climb. Pilots often minimize engine power during descent, landing, or cruising at a constant speed to conserve fuel and achieve optimal efficiency.

Throttle Management During Flight

Proper throttle management is essential to control the aircraft's speed and altitude. Pilots continuously adjust the throttle settings throughout the flight to adapt to changing flight conditions and operational requirements. During takeoff, the throttle is advanced to full power to achieve lift-off speed. After reaching a safe altitude, the pilot may reduce power to climb sustainably.

During cruise flight, the throttle is set to maintain a consistent airspeed and altitude, balancing engine power with aerodynamic forces. In descents and approaches for landing, the throttle is gradually reduced to control the descent rate and ensure a smooth touchdown.

Emergency Situations

In emergency situations, such as engine failures or the need for rapid deceleration, the throttle becomes a critical tool for managing the aircraft's energy and performance. Pilots may have to use full power to perform emergency climbs or initiate go-arounds during aborted landings. On the other hand, rapidly reducing engine power may be necessary to achieve a controlled descent in the event of engine trouble.

The throttle is a fundamental link between the pilot and the aircraft's propulsion system. Skillful manipulation of the throttle allows pilots to maintain precise control over engine power and speed, ensuring safe and efficient flight operations. Understanding the throttle's role and mastering its usage is essential for all aviators, as it empowers them to navigate the skies with confidence and proficiency.

Flaps and Their Significance During Takeoff and Landing

In this section, we explore the crucial role of flaps in aircraft operations, particularly during takeoff and landing. Flaps are movable wing surfaces that provide additional lift and control over the aircraft's flight characteristics. They play a vital role in ensuring safe and efficient takeoffs and landings, enhancing the aircraft's maneuverability during these critical phases of flight.

Understanding Flaps

Flaps are hinged sections on the trailing edge of an aircraft's wings, which the pilot can extend or retract during flight. They serve as high-lift devices, altering the wing's shape and increasing its surface area. By extending the flaps, pilots can modify the wing's camber and chord, enabling the aircraft to generate more lift at lower speeds.

Takeoff Configuration

During takeoff preparations, pilots configure the flaps to their optimum position to achieve the necessary lift at lower speeds during the initial stages of flight. The extended flaps create additional lift, allowing the aircraft to become airborne at lower rates. This is particularly crucial for shorter runways, or the aircraft's weight is near its maximum takeoff limit.

As the aircraft accelerates along the runway, the flaps generate the extra lift required to lift the plane off the ground at a safe speed. Once the aircraft is airborne and reaches a safe climbing speed, the flaps are gradually retracted to reduce drag and improve fuel efficiency during the climb phase.

Landing Configuration

During the landing phase, the flaps are pivotal in slowing down the aircraft and allowing it to descend safely for touchdown. As the pilot prepares for landing, the flaps are extended to increase lift at lower speeds, enabling the aircraft to maintain a controlled descent during the approach.

The extended flaps also help the aircraft maintain a steeper approach angle, allowing for a more precise touchdown point on the runway. By utilizing the flaps' lift-enhancing capabilities, pilots can reduce the aircraft's approach speed, making landings smoother and safer, especially during adverse weather conditions or short runways.

Different Flap Settings

Modern aircraft often have multiple flap settings, known as "flap settings" or "flap positions." Pilots can choose different degrees of flap extension based on the aircraft's weight, runway length, weather conditions, and other operational considerations.

Takeoff flaps, approach flaps, and landing flaps are standard flap settings. Takeoff flaps provide the maximum lift for the initial climb, approach flaps enhance low-speed control during the final approach, and landing flaps offer the most significant lift for a safe touchdown and rollout.

Flaps are integral to an aircraft's safe and efficient operation during takeoff and landing. By adjusting the wing's configuration, flaps provide the necessary lift at lower speeds, enabling the plane to take off and land safely. Their ability to modify the wing's shape and generate additional lift enhances the aircraft's maneuverability and control during critical phases of flight. Mastering the optimal use of flaps is a vital skill for pilots, ensuring the smooth and successful execution of takeoffs and landings and ultimately contributing to the safety and precision of flight operations.

Cockpit Instruments and Their Crucial Role in Pilot Decision-Making

In this section, we discuss the essential role of cockpit instruments in aviation and their significance in aiding pilot decision-making. Cockpit instruments are sophisticated devices that provide vital flight data, ensuring each flight's safety, efficiency, and success. They empower pilots with real-time information about the aircraft's performance, position, and environmental conditions, enabling them to make informed decisions and respond effectively to various flight situations.

The Flight Instrument Panel

The flight instrument panel, commonly known as the "cockpit," is the nerve center of an aircraft. It houses a myriad of instruments that provide critical information to the pilot. These instruments are meticulously arranged to offer quick and easy access to essential data during all phases of flight. Each device serves a specific purpose, contributing to the aircraft's overall situational awareness and control.

Primary Flight Instruments

Primary flight instruments are crucial for essential flight control and navigation. They include the following:

- **Airspeed Indicator (ASI)**: The ASI displays the aircraft's airspeed, informing the pilot of the speed relative to the surrounding air. It is vital for maintaining proper takeoff, climb, cruise, and landing speeds.
- **Attitude Indicator (AI)**: Also known as the artificial horizon, the AI displays the aircraft's pitch and roll angles relative to the Earth's horizon. It provides critical information about the aircraft's orientation and helps the pilot maintain level flight and execute turns.
- **Altimeter**: The altimeter indicates the aircraft's altitude above sea level. It aids in determining the aircraft's vertical

position and ensures safe terrain clearance during flight.

- **Heading Indicator (HI)**: The HI displays the aircraft's magnetic heading. It is a crucial navigation instrument, helping the pilot maintain the desired direction and follow assigned headings.

Additional Cockpit Instruments

In addition to the primary flight instruments, modern aircraft have many advanced instruments that offer comprehensive situational awareness. These may include:

- **Vertical Speed Indicator (VSI)**: The VSI shows the rate of climb or descent, enabling the pilot to adjust the aircraft's vertical movement.
- **Turn Coordinator**: The turn coordinator displays the rate and coordination of turns, assisting the pilot in executing coordinated and precise turns.
- **Navigation Systems**: Advanced navigation systems, such as GPS and Inertial Navigation Systems (INS), provide accurate position data and assist in route planning and tracking.
- **Weather Radar and TCAS**: Weather radar systems help identify and avoid adverse weather conditions, while Traffic Collision Avoidance System (TCAS) warns of potential air traffic conflicts.

Pilot Decision-Making

Cockpit instruments are indispensable tools for pilot decision-making. Their real-time data allows pilots to assess the aircraft's performance, track progress, and monitor environmental conditions. These instruments offer critical guidance to make informed decisions in challenging situations, such as adverse weather, turbulence, or emergency scenarios.

Pilots can maintain precise control over the aircraft by continuously cross-referencing multiple instruments and systems, ensuring safe and efficient flight operations. Cockpit instruments serve as the pilot's eyes and ears, empowering them to confidently navigate the skies and make well-informed choices, ultimately enhancing the safety and success of each flight.

5

Safety in the Skies

N ow we'll explore the critical topic of aviation safety, discussing comprehensive statistics and making meaningful comparisons with other modes of transportation. Safety is paramount in the aviation industry, and understanding the risks and safety measures is essential for industry professionals and passengers.

Aviation Safety Statistics

Aviation safety statistics provide an insightful understanding of the safety standards in the aviation industry. Despite the vast number of flights operating worldwide daily, flying remains one of the safest forms of travel. A testament to rigorous safety regulations, relentless technological advancements, and thorough training protocols, the incidence of accidents is remarkably low. While even a single accident is too many, it's worth noting that most flights reach their destination safely. Each accident, though tragic, provides valuable lessons that drive further improvements in aviation safety, reinforcing the industry's commitment to making air travel safer with each passing day.

Comparisons with Other Modes of Transport

Aviation safety is often measured in terms of accidents per distance traveled or fatalities per passenger-kilometer. To gain a comprehensive perspective, we compare aviation safety statistics with other transportation modes, such as road travel, rail travel, and maritime transport. These comparisons shed light on the relative risks associated with different forms of travel and allow us to understand the strengths and weaknesses of each transportation mode in terms of safety.

Factors Impacting Aviation Safety

To further our exploration, we analyze the various factors that impact aviation safety. These may include human factors, such as pilot error, fatigue, and training; technical factors, such as aircraft design and maintenance; environmental factors, including weather conditions and air traffic density; and operational aspects, such as air traffic control procedures and airport infrastructure. Understanding these factors is crucial for implementing effective safety measures and reducing the risk of accidents.

The Role of Aviation Regulations

Aviation safety falls under the stringent oversight of both national and international aviation regulatory bodies. This text delves into the contributions of organizations like the Federal

Aviation Administration (FAA), the International Civil Aviation Organization (ICAO), and the European Union Aviation Safety Agency (EASA), among others. These entities establish safety benchmarks, carry out audits, and supervise adherence to regulations. Furthermore, we inspect how safety directives influence elements such as aircraft design, maintenance procedures, pilot training, and air traffic management.

Advancements in Safety Technology

Technological progress significantly bolsters aviation safety, a critical aspect we explore here. Our focus is on the innovative safety technologies incorporated into modern aircraft, such as collision avoidance systems, terrain awareness and warning systems, weather radar, and state-of-the-art flight control systems. Additionally, we inspect the use of data analytics and artificial intelligence in discerning potential safety risks and augmenting operational safety.

Crisis Management and Accident Investigation

Despite stringent safety protocols, the aviation industry acknowledges that rare accidents can still occur. During such unfortunate events, well-established crisis management and accident investigation procedures are put into motion. We delve into the collaborative efforts between aviation authorities, aircraft manufacturers, and airlines in probing these accidents. Our exploration details how these entities unite to discern the root causes of accidents and subsequently enact preventive strategies to bolster safety standards. This continual investigation, learning, and improvement cycle underscores the industry's commitment to making air travel the safest possible.

Safety Culture: The Human Contribution

In conclusion, we dive into the safety culture prevalent within the aviation industry. The emphasis is on cultivating an attitude of safety-first among all stakeholders, encompassing pilots, flight attendants, ground staff, and maintenance personnel. A robust safety culture advocates a forward-thinking stance toward potential hazard detection. It fosters an environment conducive to reporting and learning from near-miss incidents.

In shedding light on aviation safety statistics, conducting insightful comparisons, and unraveling the diverse aspects of safety, our objective is to give readers a profound comprehension of the industry's devotion to safety. The continuous endeavors aimed at enhancing safety underscore the industry's resolve to maintain flying as one of the safest means of transport.

The Evolution of Aviation Safety Measures and Regulations

In this section, we embark on an intriguing voyage through the progression of aviation safety precautions and rules, retracing the steps from the initial days of flight to the advanced safety frameworks operative today. The aviation sector has made considerable strides in amplifying safety standards. Gaining insight into this developmental journey is critical to fully valuing the existing state of aviation safety.

Early Safety Measures in Aviation

At the inception of aviation, safety concerns were largely uncharted territory. The pioneers of flight faced numerous challenges as they ventured into the skies. We explore the early safety measures that aviation pioneers implemented, often involving trial and error. From rudimentary aircraft design improvements to introducing safety harnesses for pilots, we uncover the first steps taken to minimize risks in the developing world of aviation.

The Birth of Aviation Regulations

With the burgeoning popularity of aviation, the necessity for official rules and safety norms emerged. We study the pioneering aviation laws established by different nations to safeguard pilots, passengers, and the public. These preliminary rules zeroed in on aspects like aircraft build, pilot accreditation, and rudimentary operational procedures aimed at curbing accidents and lessening associated risks.

The Impact of World Wars on Aviation Safety

The outbreak of World Wars I and II brought significant advancements in aviation technology. Military conflicts spurred the development of more powerful aircraft, but safety became an even more critical concern. We analyze how wartime experiences influenced the establishment of global aviation safety standards, such as the Chicago Convention in 1944, which laid the foundation for international cooperation in regulating aviation safety.

Post-War Safety Innovations

Following World War II, the aviation industry experienced rapid growth as commercial air travel became increasingly popular. This era saw the introduction of groundbreaking safety innovations, including pressurized cabins, improved cockpit instrumentation, and advances in weather forecasting. We highlight the critical safety measures airlines and regulatory authorities adopt to ensure safe and efficient air transportation.

The Era of Jet Aviation

The 1950s brought forth the era of jet-powered aircraft, revolutionizing the air travel landscape and presenting new safety complexities. These involved managing high-speed flights, conducting transcontinental operations, and integrating advanced navigation and communication systems. During this period, comprehensive safety regulations were established, tailored to the unique demands of jet aviation, affirming the industry's commitment to ensuring passenger safety amidst rapid technological advances.

Advancements in Automation and Human Factors

The second half of the 20th century was marked by remarkable progress in aviation automation and a heightened focus on human factors. This period saw the advent of autopilot systems and advances in crew resource management (CRM). These breakthroughs significantly bolstered safety measures, diminishing the probability of human error and enhancing cockpit communication, further underlining the importance of both technological and human elements in maintaining aviation safety.

Modern Safety Management Systems

Today's aviation milieu sees safety management systems (SMS) as pivotal to fortifying safety across all operational facets. The foundations of SMS and their application in airlines, airports, and maintenance establishments are extensively employed. SMS's proactive nature underscores risk evaluation, incident reporting, and ceaseless enhancement, nurturing a pervasive safety culture throughout the aviation sector.

International Collaboration and Standardization

With air travel surpassing national frontiers, international collaboration evolved as an essential factor in maintaining uniform safety standards globally. The synergistic efforts of organizations such as the International Civil Aviation Organization (ICAO) and regional aviation authorities aim to harmonize safety regulations and cultivate a universal safety culture.

This review of historical landmarks in aviation safety norms and measures illuminates the industry's steadfast dedication to safety. It underscores how an anticipatory and progressive stance has elevated air travel to be among the safest modes of transportation in today's world.

Major Advancements in Aircraft Design and Engineering for Improved Safety

This section explores the remarkable strides made in aircraft design and engineering to enhance safety and mitigate potential risks. Over the years, aviation technology has continuously evolved, leading to innovative solutions that have significantly contributed to safer skies.

Crashworthiness and Impact Absorption

Crashworthiness is a vital facet of aircraft safety, focusing on an aircraft's capability to safeguard its occupants during a crash. The evolution of innovative materials and structural designs that effectively absorb and distribute the forces generated during a collision has been paramount in minimizing the impact on passengers and crew. Exploring these safety-enhancing strategies spans reinforced airframes, energy-absorbing seats, and robust cabin structures, all meticulously designed to augment crash survivability. In a continuous pursuit of safety, these efforts reflect the industry's commitment to protecting lives even in the most unforeseen and unfortunate circumstances.

Enhanced Ground Proximity Warning Systems (EGPWS)

Safe navigation in challenging terrain and harsh weather conditions is fundamental to aviation safety. The evolution of Enhanced Ground Proximity Warning Systems (EGPWS) stands as a testament to the strides made in this direction. EGPWS employs state-of-the-art sensors and comprehensive databases to notify pilots of imminent hazards. These could range from rugged terrain and obstacles to unstable approaches, all posing substantial risks during critical flight stages. EGPWS plays a pivotal role in preventing accidents and securing the safety of passengers, crew, and aircraft by providing accurate and timely alerts. The advent of such sophisticated systems highlights the relentless quest of the aviation industry to blend technology with safety needs, ensuring seamless and secure flight experiences.

Terrain Awareness and Warning Systems (TAWS)

Building upon EGPWS, we investigate Terrain Awareness and Warning Systems (TAWS), which provide pilots with real-time terrain information and alerts to avoid inadvertent flight into hazardous areas. TAWS has significantly reduced the occurrence of controlled flight into terrain (CFIT) accidents, substantially impacting aviation safety.

Composite Materials and Weight Reduction

The evolution of composite materials has profoundly reshaped aircraft design, engendering lighter and stronger airframes. Carbon fiber-reinforced polymers, among other composites, have found extensive use in this domain. Adopting these materials has yielded tremendous benefits, including improved fuel efficiency and augmented structural integrity stand out. By incorporating these composites, aircraft are rendered more resistant to different stressors and fatigue, substantially increasing their durability and lifespan. This transformation illustrates the symbiosis between material science and aviation, where innovations in one area fuel advancements in the other. The result is a new generation of aircraft that not only perform better but are also safer and more efficient, underscoring the unwavering dedication of the aviation industry to continuous improvement and enhancement of safety standards.

Advanced Avionics and Automation

The advent of cutting-edge avionics and automation systems has significantly enhanced aviation safety. Features such as high-resolution weather radar and turbulence detection tools offer real-time data to aid pilots in navigating challenging weather conditions. Meanwhile, automation features like autothrottle and auto-landing capabilities ensure accurate and efficient operation of the aircraft during critical phases of flight. Collectively, these innovations contribute to a safer flying environment by assisting pilots in their decision-making processes and reducing the potential for human error, thereby elevating the safety benchmarks of aviation.

Aircraft Health Monitoring and Predictive Maintenance

The inception of Aircraft Health Monitoring (AHM) systems has facilitated the real-time surveillance of various aircraft systems and components. AHM, when synergized with predictive maintenance algorithms, aids in the early identification of possible malfunctions. This innovation supports proactive maintenance, circumventing potential in-flight interruptions and bolstering safety. It's a shift from the traditional, scheduled maintenance approach to a more efficient and predictive one, enhancing operational reliability and overall flight safety.

Redundancy and Triple Redundancy Systems

Aircraft manufacturers have engineered redundancy and triple redundancy into critical systems to bolster system reliability. This implies that multiple independent systems function concurrently, guaranteeing continued operation even in the event of a single system's failure. Such design principle introduces an additional tier of safety in contemporary aircraft, reinforcing the fault-tolerance in flight-critical systems and thereby augmenting the resilience of the aircraft against possible malfunctions.

Exploring these significant advancements highlights the aviation industry's steadfast dedication to advancing aircraft design and engineering, primarily focusing on passenger and crew safety. The continuous pursuit of innovation has resulted in cutting-edge technologies that have revolutionized air travel, making flying safer. By prioritizing crashworthiness, employing fly-by-wire technology, enhancing warning systems, utilizing advanced materials, and implementing robust avionics and automation, the skies have become a realm of increased confidence for millions of passengers worldwide. These safety strides demonstrate the industry's unwavering commitment to excellence and serve as a testament to the collaborative efforts of engineers, manufacturers, regulators, and aviation professionals who strive to make every flight a secure and reassuring experience. As the aviation journey progresses, the focus on safety remains at the forefront, ensuring that the horizon of air travel continues to soar with unparalleled security and assurance.

The Critical Role of Pilot Training and Human Factors in Aviation Safety

While technological advancements and aircraft design are pivotal in enhancing aviation safety, the human element remains equally crucial. Pilot training and understanding human factors have become integral components in ensuring safe flights.

Comprehensive Training Programs

Modern pilot training programs encompass extensive theoretical and practical modules designed to equip pilots with the knowledge and skills to handle various flight scenarios. These programs cover aircraft systems, emergency procedures, and flight simulations, enabling pilots to develop a deep understanding of their aircraft and its capabilities.

Simulator Training

Flight simulators offer a controlled and immersive environment for pilots to practice complex maneuvers, challenging weather conditions, and emergency situations. Simulator-based training allows pilots to gain experience without real-world risks, thus enhancing their decision-making skills and ability to handle unexpected events.

Continuous Learning and Recurrent Training

Aviation authorities mandate recurrent training for pilots to maintain proficiency and stay up-to-date with the latest procedures and regulations. Regular training ensures that pilots remain competent and confident in handling their aircraft, no matter their level of experience.

Crew Resource Management (CRM)

CRM emphasizes effective communication, teamwork, and

decision-making within the cockpit. It encourages a collaborative approach wherein all crew members actively contribute to the safe operation of the flight. CRM training fosters a positive cockpit culture with paramount open communication and mutual respect.

Understanding Human Factors

Human factors refer to studying how human behavior, capabilities, and limitations interact with the complex aviation environment. Recognizing the impact of fatigue, stress, workload, and situational awareness on pilot performance helps identify potential risks and implement strategies to mitigate them.

Fatigue Management

Pilots' work schedules are carefully regulated to prevent fatigue, as tiredness can impair decision-making and reaction times. Airlines adhere to strict duty hour limitations to ensure that pilots have adequate rest between flights and are trained to recognize signs of fatigue and take appropriate action.

Safety Culture

An influential safety culture is cultivated within airlines and flight organizations to prioritize safety above all else. This culture encourages reporting safety-related issues without fear of reprisal. It fosters a learning environment where accidents and incidents are thoroughly analyzed to prevent future occurrences.

The aviation industry strives to create a cohesive safety net that complements technological advancements by focusing on pilot training and understanding human factors. The synergy between advanced technology and competent, well-trained pilots ensures the skies remain safe for passengers and crew alike. As aviation continues to evolve, the commitment to comprehensive training and human-centered safety measures remains paramount in pursuing an even safer and more secure aviation landscape.

Future Challenges and Innovations in Aviation Safety

As aviation continues to advance, new challenges and opportunities arise to ensure the highest levels of safety for passengers and crew. The aviation industry continually seeks innovative solutions to address these challenges and enhance safety measures.

Integration of Artificial Intelligence (AI)

Advancements in artificial intelligence hold immense promise for aviation safety. AI-powered systems can analyze vast amounts of data in real time, enabling proactive risk assessment and predictive maintenance. Additionally, AI can aid in developing more sophisticated flight simulators that replicate real-world scenarios with greater accuracy, further enhancing pilot training.

Unmanned Aircraft Systems (UAS) Safety

Integrating automated aircraft systems, or drones, into the

airspace presents unique safety considerations. Ensuring the safe coexistence of traditional crewed aircraft and drones requires the development of robust collision-avoidance systems and comprehensive regulations to govern their operation.

Cybersecurity

With the increasing reliance on digital systems in modern aircraft, cybersecurity becomes a critical aspect of aviation safety. Protecting aircraft from cyber threats and potential hacking attempts is essential to maintain the integrity of flight-critical systems and ensure the safety of onboard passengers and crew.

Electric and Hybrid Aircraft

The emergence of electric and hybrid aircraft introduces novel safety challenges and opportunities. These aircraft rely on advanced battery technologies, necessitating the development of safety protocols for battery management and thermal control. Additionally, integrating new propulsion systems requires thorough testing and validation to ensure their reliability and safety in all operating conditions.

Sustainable Aviation Fuel (SAF) Safety

As the aviation industry endeavors to reduce its environmental impact, sustainable aviation fuel (SAF) is gaining traction. The safety implications of using alternative fuels and their compatibility with existing aircraft systems require careful evaluation and certification processes to guarantee safe and efficient operations.

Supersonic and Hypersonic Flight

The revival of interest in supersonic and hypersonic flight introduces new safety considerations. Flying at such high speeds requires advanced aerodynamics and thermal protection systems. Ensuring the safety of these aircraft during takeoff, flight, and re-entry poses unique challenges that demand innovative engineering solutions.

Urban Air Mobility (UAM)

The concept of urban air mobility, which envisions autonomous flying vehicles for short-distance transportation within urban areas, raises questions about airspace management and collision avoidance. Implementing reliable traffic management systems and integrating UAM into existing airspace infrastructure is critical to ensuring safe operations.

Global Collaboration and Data Sharing

Addressing future safety challenges requires global collaboration and data sharing among aviation stakeholders. Industry-wide transparency in reporting safety incidents and sharing lessons learned enhances the collective understanding of potential risks. It fosters a culture of continuous safety improvement.

By embracing innovation and collaboration, the aviation industry remains dedicated to confronting future safety challenges head-on. Aviation will continue to soar into a safer and more sustainable future by developing and implementing cutting-edge technologies, comprehensive regulations, and a commitment to continuous improvement.

6

The Environmental Impact of Aviation

A viation, while an incredible feat of human engineering and ingenuity, significantly impacts the environment. As airplanes operate on fossil fuels, they emit various pollutants into the atmosphere, contributing to climate change and environmental degradation. This section discusses the environmental implications of airplane emissions, shedding light on the challenges faced by the aviation industry in mitigating its carbon footprint.

Greenhouse Gas Emissions

Airplanes emit greenhouse gases, including carbon dioxide (CO_2), nitrous oxide (N_2O), and water vapor. CO_2 is the most concerning greenhouse gas, accounting for a significant portion of aviation's impact on climate change. These emissions trap heat in the Earth's atmosphere, leading to global warming and adverse effects on ecosystems, weather patterns, and sea levels.

Contrails and Cirrus Cloud Formation

In addition to greenhouse gases, airplanes produce contrails – the visible trails of condensed water vapor left behind as exhaust gases cool at high altitudes. Contrails can persist for hours and contribute to the formation of cirrus clouds, which trap heat in the atmosphere and exacerbate the greenhouse effect.

Nitrogen Oxide (NOx) Emissions

Airplane engines also emit nitrogen oxides (NOx), contributing to ground-level ozone formation and air pollution. NOx emissions near airports can have adverse health effects on nearby communities and worsen air quality.

Noise Pollution

Apart from emissions, aircraft generate noise pollution during takeoff and landing. Aircraft noise can disturb communities surrounding airports, impacting wildlife, sleep patterns, and overall quality of life for residents.

Sustainable Aviation Fuel (SAF) and Alternative Technologies

The aviation industry is actively exploring sustainable alternatives to address these environmental challenges. Sustainable aviation fuel (SAF) – produced from renewable sources – potentially reduces greenhouse gas emissions. Additionally, advancements in electric and hybrid aircraft technologies promise to lower emissions and noise levels.

Carbon Offsetting and Emission Reduction Initiatives

Airline operators and organizations are increasingly embracing carbon offsetting and emission reduction initiatives to counter-balance the environmental impact of air travel. These initiatives involve investing in projects that sequester or reduce equivalent CO_2 emissions to offset the emissions generated during flights.

International Agreements and Regulations

The aviation industry collaborates internationally to establish environmental standards and regulations. Agreements such as the International Civil Aviation Organization's (ICAO) Carbon Offsetting and Reduction Scheme for International Aviation (CORSIA) aim to achieve carbon-neutral growth in international aviation.

Future Sustainability Goals

As the industry moves forward, the aviation sector aims to achieve ambitious sustainability goals. These include the development of zero-emission aircraft, increased SAF usage, and the integrating of new technologies to reduce environmental impact significantly.

The aviation industry must seek greener and more sustainable practices to understand the environmental consequences of airplane emissions. Efforts to reduce greenhouse gas emissions, noise pollution, and other environmental impacts are essential in preserving the skies we soar through while mitigating the industry's contribution to climate change and ecological disturbances.

Greenhouse Gases and Their Contribution to Climate Change

Greenhouse gases (GHGs) are central to climate change, and aviation significantly contributes to their emissions. This section discusses the impact of greenhouse gases on the Earth's climate. It highlights the role of the aviation industry in contributing to this global environmental challenge.

Understanding Greenhouse Gases

Greenhouse gases trap heat in the Earth's atmosphere, creating a natural greenhouse effect necessary for maintaining a habitable climate. The primary greenhouse gases include carbon dioxide (CO_2), methane (CH_4), nitrous oxide (N_2O), and fluorinated gases. While some GHGs occur naturally, human activities, including aviation, have significantly increased atmospheric concentrations.

The Aviation Sector's Greenhouse Gas Emissions

Aviation is responsible for a substantial share of global greenhouse gas emissions. CO_2 emissions from burning jet fuel are the most significant contributors, accounting for approximately 2% of global emissions. However, considering other factors like contrail and cirrus cloud formation, aviation's overall climate impact could be higher.

High Altitude Emissions and the Climate Forcing Effect

Airplanes emit GHGs at high altitudes, where their impact on the climate is more potent. At these altitudes, emissions have a more significant "climate forcing" effect, exacerbating their warming potential than ground-level emissions.

The Carbon-Climate Feedback Loop

Greenhouse gas emissions from aviation and other sources contribute to the rise of global temperatures. As the Earth's temperature increases, it triggers various climate feedback mechanisms, such as melting polar ice and permafrost, which release stored methane and carbon dioxide, intensifying the greenhouse effect.

Impacts on Weather Patterns and Extreme Events

The increase in greenhouse gases influences weather patterns. It contributes to extreme weather events, including heatwaves, droughts, hurricanes, and heavy rainfall. These events have far-reaching consequences for ecosystems, agriculture, and human communities.

Addressing Aviation's Climate Impact

The aviation industry recognizes the urgency of reducing greenhouse gas emissions to curb climate change. Sustainable aviation fuels (SAF), aircraft efficiency improvements, and air traffic management advancements are among the strategies to mitigate aviation's environmental footprint.

The Role of International Collaboration

Addressing climate change requires a global effort. International organizations, governments, and aviation stakeholders collaborate to develop policies and agreements that promote carbon-neutral growth and emission reduction targets for the aviation sector.

The Need for Climate-Resilient Air Transport

In addition to mitigating its emissions, the aviation industry is adapting to climate change's impacts. Ensuring climate-resilient air transport systems is essential to cope with changing weather patterns and potential disruptions to flight operations.

By understanding the significance of greenhouse gases and their role in climate change, the aviation industry is better equipped to address its environmental impact proactively. As aviation continues to evolve, a strong commitment to reducing emissions, fostering innovation, and adopting sustainable practices is paramount in building a more environmentally responsible future for air travel.

The Role of Aviation in Cloud Formation and Ozone Concentrations

Besides greenhouse gas emissions, aviation has a noteworthy impact on cloud formation and ozone concentrations in the Earth's atmosphere. This section highlights the intricate relationship between aviation activities and these atmospheric phenomena.

Contrail Formation

Contrails, short for "condensation trails," are the visible lines of cloud-like trails left by aircraft in their wake. These trails form when hot engine exhaust gases mix with the colder surrounding air at high altitudes. Contrails consist of ice crystals and can persist for several hours, spreading and transforming into cirrus-like clouds. As air traffic increases, contrail formation becomes more prevalent, influencing cloud cover and atmospheric dynamics.

Contrail Cirrus Clouds

Contrail cirrus clouds are a specific cloud formation triggered by persistent contrails. These clouds have a net warming effect on the Earth's climate, trapping outgoing infrared radiation and contributing to a positive radiative forcing. Research suggests that the climate impact of contrail cirrus clouds may be more significant than carbon dioxide emissions alone.

Aviation's Effect on Ozone Concentrations

Ozone (O_3) is a crucial component of the Earth's atmosphere, present both in the stratosphere and the troposphere. While ozone in the stratosphere is beneficial as it protects life on Earth from harmful ultraviolet radiation, ozone in the troposphere is a greenhouse gas and a pollutant. Aviation contributes to ozone formation in the troposphere through aircraft engine nitrogen oxide (NOx) emissions. These emissions can produce ozone, especially near airports and high-traffic air routes.

Nitrogen Oxides (NOx) and Ozone Depletion

Although ozone concentrations in the troposphere are harmful, NOx emissions from aviation can also impact the stratospheric ozone layer. High-altitude aircraft release NOx, which can eventually reach the stratosphere and participate in chemical reactions that deplete ozone. However, compared to other sources of NOx emissions, aviation's contribution to stratospheric ozone depletion remains relatively small.

Stratospheric Aviation and Ozone Layer Impact

Supersonic aircraft, such as the Concorde, operate at altitudes near the stratosphere, where they can release nitrogen oxides directly into this sensitive layer. The impact of stratospheric aviation on ozone depletion has been a subject of research and regulatory consideration.

Mitigating Aviation's Effect on Clouds and Ozone

The aviation industry acknowledges the importance of addressing its impact on cloud formation and ozone concentrations. Research is ongoing to understand the complexities of contrail formation and cirrus cloud behavior. Additionally, advances in aircraft technology and air traffic management can help reduce contrail formation and minimize the emission of ozone-forming pollutants.

Balancing Environmental Impact and Advancements

As aviation progresses, a delicate balance must be struck between technological advancements and minimizing environmental consequences. Collaborative efforts between aviation stakeholders, researchers, and environmental organizations are crucial in finding sustainable solutions to mitigate aviation's effects on clouds and ozone concentrations.

By comprehending aviation's multifaceted role in cloud formation and ozone concentrations, the industry can minimize its impact on the atmosphere and contribute to global efforts in environmental stewardship.

The Quest for Greener Skies: Innovations and Future Directions

As the world faces increasing concerns about climate change and environmental sustainability, the aviation industry is committed to pushing the boundaries of innovation to achieve greener skies. This section delves into the ongoing quest for sustainable aviation. It highlights the promising innovations and future directions that aim to reduce the environmental impact of air travel.

Advanced Sustainable Fuels

Researchers and industry experts continuously explore advanced sustainable fuels beyond the current Sustainable Aviation Fuels (SAFs) generation. These next-generation fuels may include power-to-liquid (PtL) energies produced by converting renewable electricity into synthetic aviation fuels. Innovative biofuel feedstocks and conversion processes can increase SAF production and contribute to a more sustainable aviation ecosystem.

Electric Aviation Advancements

Electric aviation is at the forefront of sustainable technology, and the industry is investing heavily in advancing electric propulsion systems. Researchers are developing more efficient and energy-dense batteries, enabling longer-range electric flights. Furthermore, rapid progress is being made in hybrid-electric aircraft, which combine electric and conventional propulsion systems to optimize efficiency and extend flight capabilities.

Hydrogen-Powered Flight

Hydrogen continues to be a promising energy carrier for aviation, and research into hydrogen-powered aircraft is gaining momentum. Developing hydrogen fuel cells and more efficient storage solutions could revolutionize the industry, offering a zero-emission alternative for long-haul flights. Hydrogen infrastructure, including production, distribution, and refueling, is also a focal point to support the widespread adoption of hydrogen-powered aviation.

Sustainable Airports

Airports are essential to the aviation system, and efforts to achieve greener skies extend to airport operations. Many airports are implementing renewable energy sources, such as solar panels and wind turbines, to power facilities and reduce carbon emissions. Additionally, airport design and sustainable infrastructure advancements are crucial in minimizing the overall environmental impact of air travel.

Urban Air Mobility Integration

Urban Air Mobility (UAM) concepts are gaining traction as a means of reducing urban congestion and emissions. Electric Vertical Takeoff and Landing (eVTOL) aircraft could revolution-ize urban transportation, providing a greener and more efficient alternative for short-distance commuting. Integrating UAM into urban landscapes requires careful planning and cooperation with regulatory bodies to ensure safe and sustainable operations.

Sustainable Aviation Policy and Regulations

Government agencies and international organizations play a pivotal role in shaping the future of sustainable aviation. Establishing robust policies and regulations that incentivize the adoption of green technologies and practices is vital. Collaboration between governments, industry stakeholders, and environmental experts is crucial to create a cohesive framework that supports sustainable aviation development.

Global Collaboration and Partnerships

Pursuing greener skies requires a collective effort from the global aviation community. Collaborative research and development initiatives, public-private partnerships, and knowledge-sharing platforms foster innovation and accelerate the implementation of sustainable solutions. Multinational cooperation is essential to address the complex challenges of sustainable aviation on a global scale.

The quest for greener skies is a dynamic and evolving journey driven by the shared commitment of aviation industry stake-holders, researchers, policymakers, and environmental advocates. With a focus on continuous innovation and sustainable practices, the aviation sector aims to shape a future where air travel is efficient, safe, and environmentally responsible, preserving the skies for future generations.

7

Beyond Earth's Boundaries: Exploration and Spaceflight

The Transition from Aviation to Spaceflight

As humanity's fascination with the skies soared to new heights, a natural progression led to space exploration, marking the transition from aviation to spaceflight. This chapter explores the remarkable journey of venturing beyond Earth's boundaries and the pioneering efforts that propelled us into the cosmos.

The Dawn of Space Age

The space age dawned on October 4, 1957, with the launch of Sputnik 1, the world's first artificial satellite, by the Soviet Union. This historic event ignited the space race between the United States and the Soviet Union, setting the stage for human space exploration and scientific advancements.

Mercury and Vostok Programs

In the early 1960s, the United States and the Soviet Union launched human spaceflight programs. The Mercury program, led by NASA, aimed to send American astronauts into space. Meanwhile, the Soviet Vostok program achieved groundbreaking milestones, such as Yuri Gagarin becoming the first human to orbit Earth in 1961.

The Apollo Missions

The iconic Apollo program became the pinnacle of human spaceflight, symbolizing humanity's quest to reach the Moon. On July 20, 1969, NASA's Apollo 11 mission achieved a momentous feat as Neil Armstrong and Buzz Aldrin became the first humans to set foot on the lunar surface.

Space Shuttle Era

The Space Shuttle program revolutionized space travel, enabling reusable spacecraft to transport astronauts and payloads into orbit. For over three decades, the space shuttle fleet facilitated numerous missions, including satellite deployment, space station construction, and scientific research.

International Space Station (ISS)

A symbol of international cooperation, the ISS is a state-of-the-art space laboratory that orbits Earth and is a platform for scientific experiments and research. It brings together astronauts from different countries, fostering collaboration and advancing our understanding of space.

Robotic Space Exploration

Robotic probes and rovers have explored distant planets, moons, and celestial bodies parallel with crewed missions. Landmark missions include the Voyager probes, which ventured beyond our solar system, and the Mars rovers, which continue to unveil the mysteries of the Red Planet.

Commercial Spaceflight

The emergence of private space companies, such as SpaceX, Blue Origin, and Virgin Galactic, has revolutionized space access. Commercial spaceflight endeavors aim to make space travel more accessible to the public and facilitate commercial satellite launches and resupply missions to the ISS.

Future of Human Space Exploration

Humanity's journey into space is far from over. Exciting and ambitious plans loom ahead, encompassing NASA's Artemis program, which aims to return to the Moon and venture into Mars with crewed missions. Advancements in propulsion, life support systems, and sustainable space habitats are critical to these bold endeavors.

The transition from aviation to spaceflight represents a pivotal moment in human history as we ventured beyond Earth's atmosphere to explore the cosmos. With each mission and breakthrough, we expand our knowledge, push the boundaries of technology, and embrace the boundless possibilities that await us among the stars.

The Challenges of Supersonic and Hypersonic Flight at the Edge of Space

As the frontiers of exploration extend beyond Earth's atmosphere, the pursuit of supersonic and hypersonic flight at the edge of space presents a unique set of challenges and opportunities. This section discusses the thrilling realm of high-speed flight, where aircraft push the boundaries of aerodynamics and engineering to conquer the skies.

Breaking the Sound Barrier

Supersonic flight, defined as exceeding the speed of sound (approximately 767 mph or 1,235 km/h at sea level), revolutionized aviation during the mid-20th century. The iconic Bell X-1, piloted by Chuck Yeager, became the first crewed aircraft to break the sound barrier in 1947, opening new possibilities for faster and more efficient air travel.

The Sonic Boom Dilemma

Supersonic flight is accompanied by a phenomenon known as the sonic boom, a shockwave created as the aircraft exceeds the speed of sound. The disruptive noise generated by the sonic boom raised concerns about its impact on populated areas, leading to regulations restricting supersonic flight over land.

The Rise of Hypersonic Flight

Hypersonic flight, defined as flying at speeds greater than Mach 5 (approximately 3,836 mph or 6,174 km/h), represents the next frontier in high-speed aviation. Hypersonic vehicles operate at extreme temperatures and encounter intense aerodynamic forces, requiring innovative materials and engineering solutions.

The Thermal Challenge

As aircraft reach hypersonic speeds, they encounter significant aerodynamic heating caused by friction with the atmosphere. Overcoming this thermal challenge demands advanced thermal protection systems to shield the vehicle and its occupants from extreme temperatures.

Aerodynamics and Stability

At hypersonic speeds, aircraft face complex aerodynamic issues, including shockwaves, boundary layer interactions, and wave drag. Achieving stability and control becomes paramount in this regime, demanding sophisticated flight control systems and design configurations.

Material Science Advancements

Hypersonic flight places enormous stress on the aircraft's structure and surfaces. Advancements in material science, such as high-temperature ceramics and composite materials, play a crucial role in ensuring the vehicle's structural integrity and safety.

Future Applications

Hypersonic flight holds promise for various applications, from rapid global travel to military surveillance and space access. The development of hypersonic vehicles may revolutionize transportation and enable faster intercontinental journeys.

Balancing Speed and Efficiency

While high-speed flight offers unprecedented efficiency for long-haul travel, it must be balanced with environmental considerations. Addressing the ecological impact of hypersonic and supersonic flight, including emissions and noise pollution, remains a significant challenge.

As aviation ventures into supersonic and hypersonic flight at the edge of space, engineers, scientists, and researchers collaborate to overcome technical hurdles and unlock the full potential of high-speed travel. With ongoing advancements, the dream of rapid and efficient air travel, even beyond Earth's boundaries, inspires a new generation of explorers and visionaries.

The Legacy of Lifting Bodies and Their Role in Early Space Exploration

During the pioneering era of space exploration, lifting bodies were pivotal in advancing our understanding of atmospheric re-entry and spacecraft design. This section delves into these unique aerospace vehicles' fascinating history and enduring legacy.

A New Concept in Aerodynamics

Lifting bodies represented a departure from traditional space-craft designs. Unlike capsules, which relied solely on parachutes for re-entry, lifting bodies utilized their aerodynamic shape to generate lift and control their descent through the Earth's atmosphere.

Early Experiments

The concept of lifting bodies emerged in the late 1950s and early 1960s, driven by the need to develop more controllable and reusable spacecraft. NASA's Flight Research Center (now Armstrong Flight Research Center) and other organizations embarked on experimental flights to test the feasibility of this new design.

X-Series Lifting Body Program

NASA's X-series of lifting body experiments included iconic vehicles such as the M2-F1, HL-10, and X-24. These experimental aircraft demonstrated the viability of aerodynamic lift during re-entry, paving the way for future spacecraft designs.

Flight Testing and Lessons Learned

The flight tests of lifting bodies provided valuable insights into aerodynamic stability, control systems, and heat protection during re-entry. Lessons learned from these trials influenced the development of future space shuttle and spacecraft programs.

The Space Shuttle Era

The legacy of lifting bodies found its ultimate expression in the Space Shuttle program. NASA's Space Shuttle, with its delta-winged orbiter, incorporated lifting body principles to enhance its re-entry capabilities and glide to a precise landing.

Reusability and Cost-Effectiveness

Lifting bodies demonstrated the potential for reusability in spacecraft design, an essential feature for reducing the cost of space missions. The lessons learned from lifting body experiments contributed to reusable space shuttle technology development.

Advancements in Re-Entry Technology

The knowledge gained from lifting body research influenced advancements in thermal protection systems, enabling spacecraft to endure the extreme heat of re-entry. This progress significantly enhanced crew safety during atmospheric re-entry.

Lifting Body Contributions to Space Exploration

Beyond Earth's atmosphere, the principles of lifting bodies influenced the design of spacecraft destined for other planets and celestial bodies. The Mars Science Laboratory (Curiosity rover) and the SpaceX Dragon capsule are examples of vehicles that apply lifting body concepts for atmospheric entry and landing.

Inspiring Future Aerospace Innovations

The legacy of lifting bodies inspires aerospace engineers and scientists to explore innovative spacecraft designs for future missions. Concepts like the Dream Chaser and other lifting body-inspired vehicles illustrate the enduring impact of these early experiments.

As we reflect on the legacy of lifting bodies, we recognize their indispensable contribution to early space exploration and their lasting influence on spacecraft design and re-entry technology. These daring experiments challenged conventional thinking and paved the way for the remarkable achievements of modern space missions, inspiring generations of space explorers to reach even greater heights.

The Future of Aerospace Technology: Spaceplanes and Reusable Spacecraft

With the continuous evolution of space exploration, aerospace technology is relentlessly pushing the limits of what humanity can achieve. This segment explores the captivating realm of spaceplanes and reusable spacecraft, revealing the promising breakthroughs that have the potential to revolutionize space travel.

The Rise of Spaceplanes

Spaceplanes, also known as reusable space vehicles, are a new generation of spacecraft designed to combine the capabilities of traditional rockets and airplanes. Unlike expendable rockets, spaceplanes can return to Earth and be relaunched, offering significant cost savings and increased mission flexibility.

Reusable Launch Vehicles (RLVs)

Space agencies and private aerospace companies are actively developing RLVs to make space travel more sustainable and affordable. SpaceX's Falcon 9 and Falcon Heavy, Blue Origin's New Shepard, and Virgin Galactic's SpaceShipTwo are prominent examples of RLVs aiming to revolutionize space access.

Vertical Takeoff and Landing (VTOL) Spaceplanes

Like helicopters, VTOL spaceplanes represent an exciting subcategory that can take off and land vertically. These vehicles eliminate the need for extensive launch infrastructure and open up possibilities for launching missions from various locations.

Single-Stage-to-Orbit (SSTO) Concepts

Advancements in propulsion and materials have renewed interest in SSTO concepts, which aim to reach orbit without jettisoning any significant components. The development of SSTO vehicles could streamline space access and reduce the complexity of launch systems.

Suborbital Space Tourism

Reusable spacecraft are making space tourism a reality, allowing civilians to experience the thrill of space travel. Companies like Virgin Galactic and Blue Origin are pioneering suborbital space tourism, opening up a new era of commercial space ventures.

Advantages of Reusability

The reusability of spaceplanes offers several advantages, including reduced manufacturing costs, quicker turnaround times between missions, and the potential for increased payload capacity. This disruptive technology has the potential to reshape the economics of space travel.

Sustainable Space Exploration

As space exploration extends beyond low Earth orbit, reusable spacecraft become essential for sustainable missions to the Moon, Mars, and beyond. Their ability to return to Earth and be refueled, refurbished, and relaunched promises to unlock new possibilities in space exploration.

Challenges and Opportunities

Developing spaceplanes and reusable spacecraft has challenges, including engineering complexities, safety considerations, and technological advancements. However, the rewards of more accessible and sustainable space travel make these endeavors worthwhile.

A New Era of Space Exploration

With spaceplanes and reusable spacecraft on the horizon, the aerospace industry stands on the brink of a new era in space exploration. As these technologies mature, we can anticipate exciting missions, scientific discoveries, and expanding human presence in space.

As we peer into the future of aerospace technology, spaceplanes, and reusable spacecraft offer a glimpse into a world where space travel is more accessible, economically viable, and environmentally conscious. These innovations carry the potential to transform our understanding of the cosmos and inspire a new generation of spacefarers to reach for the stars.

Collaborative Efforts in Space Exploration: Past, Present, and Future Missions

Collaboration has been a cornerstone of space exploration, bringing together multiple nations' and organizations' expertise, resources, and aspirations to achieve remarkable milestones beyond Earth. This section examines the history, current endeavors, and future prospects of collaborative efforts in space exploration.

International Space Station (ISS)

The International Space Station stands as a shining example of international cooperation in space. Constructed through joint efforts by NASA, Roscosmos, ESA, JAXA, and CSA, the ISS serves as a microgravity laboratory and a testament to the peaceful collaboration between nations.

Scientific Partnerships

Collaborative missions extend beyond the ISS, with various

countries teaming up to explore celestial bodies and conduct cutting-edge research. For instance, the Mars Rover missions, such as NASA's Perseverance and ESA's ExoMars, involve contributions from multiple space agencies and scientific institutions.

Lunar Exploration Consortia

The Moon has become a focal point for global cooperation in space exploration. The Artemis program, led by NASA, aims to return astronauts to the lunar surface, and it involves partnerships with international space agencies, paving the way for sustainable lunar exploration.

Joint Space Telescopes

Telescopes such as the Hubble Space Telescope and the James Webb Space Telescope have been collaborative efforts, uniting multiple nations' scientific and technological prowess to peer deep into the cosmos.

Space Exploration Initiatives in Developing Nations

Collaboration in space exploration is expanding beyond traditional spacefaring nations. Developing countries are increasingly forging partnerships with established space agencies to build their capabilities and contribute to global space endeavors.

Sharing Data and Expertise

Collaborative missions often involve sharing data, research findings, and technical know-how. This exchange of information accelerates scientific progress and fosters a spirit of openness and cooperation among spacefaring nations.

Space Diplomacy

Collaborative space missions have the potential to promote diplomatic relations and foster peaceful interactions between countries. Space exploration can serve as a unifying force, transcending geopolitical boundaries and advancing humanity's shared quest for knowledge.

Future Collaborative Space Missions

As space exploration ventures into deeper space and ambitious endeavors like crewed missions to Mars become realistic goals, collaboration is expected to play an even more significant role. Partnerships between nations, private companies, and international organizations will be crucial for undertaking complex missions beyond Earth.

Challenges and Benefits of Collaboration

While collaboration brings immense benefits, it also presents challenges, including differences in technological standards, regulatory frameworks, and cultural norms. Overcoming these hurdles requires open communication, mutual understanding, and a shared commitment to exploration.

Global Space Cooperation

The future of space exploration lies in global space cooperation, where nations pool their expertise and resources to tackle humanity's most profound questions about the universe. Together, we can continue pushing the boundaries of space exploration, advancing scientific knowledge, and expanding the human presence beyond our home planet.

In the spirit of unity and cooperation, collaborative efforts in space exploration have repeatedly proven that we are stronger. From the International Space Station to upcoming missions to the Moon and Mars, the collective pursuit of knowledge and discovery will lead humanity to new frontiers and unlock the mysteries of the cosmos.

8

The People Behind the Wings: Notable Aviators and Innovators

Pioneers of Aviation: The Wright Brothers and Their Achievements

The history of aviation is inseparable from the remarkable contributions of the Wright brothers, Orville and Wilbur. Born in the late 19th century, their passion for flight ignited an era of innovation and forever changed the course of human transportation. This section explores the lives and achievements of these aviation pioneers, shedding light on their incredible journey to conquer the skies.

Early Life and Passion for Flight

Orville and Wilbur Wright grew up in Dayton, Ohio, in a family that fostered curiosity and ingenuity. Their interest in mechanics and engineering was evident from a young age, setting the stage for their future endeavors in aviation.

Pursuing the Dream of Flight

Inspired by the works of early aviation pioneers and a fascination with the flight of birds, the Wright brothers became determined to build a flying machine. Their quest for the impossible began with extensive research on the principles of aerodynamics and aircraft control.

The First Powered Flight

On December 17, 1903, in Kitty Hawk, North Carolina, the Wright brothers achieved what was once deemed impossible—the first sustained, controlled, powered flight. Orville piloted the aircraft Flyer I for 12 seconds, covering a distance of 120 feet, marking a momentous leap in human history.

Continuous Innovation

The success of their initial flight only fueled their dedication to advancing aviation. The Wright brothers continued refining their aircraft, improving stability and control mechanisms, and making longer and more impressive flights.

The Wright Flyer III

In 1905, the Wright brothers designed the Flyer III, which featured a revolutionary three-axis control system. This breakthrough allowed the pilot to control the airplane's pitch, roll, and yaw, making it controllable in flight.

Sharing Knowledge

Unlike some contemporaries, the Wright brothers were open about their work and shared their findings with other aviators and institutions. This collaborative approach contributed significantly to the rapid development of aviation worldwide.

Legacy of Innovation

The Wright brothers' relentless pursuit of flight laid the foundation for modern aviation. Their innovative concepts, such as wing warping and the three-axis control system, became fundamental principles in aircraft design.

Impact on Aviation

The success of the Wright brothers' early flights sparked global interest in aviation. It inspired a new generation of aviators, engineers, and inventors. Their achievements served as a catalyst for further advancements in aeronautics and aerospace technology.

Recognition and Honors

Over time, the Wright brothers received recognition and accolades for their groundbreaking accomplishments. Their achievements have been commemorated through numerous museums, memorials, and aviation awards worldwide.

Inspiring Future Generations

Beyond their historical significance, the Wright brothers' story inspires aspiring aviators and scientists. Their determination, courage, and unwavering belief in the human potential show-case the power of innovation and the boundless possibilities that await those who dare to dream.

In the chronicles of human history, the names of Orville and Wilbur Wright stand as a testament to human ingenuity and the indomitable spirit of exploration. Their pursuit of flight paved the way for the modern aerospace industry and forever changed the world. The Wright brothers' legacy lives on, soaring above the horizon as a beacon of human achievement and a testament to the unyielding pursuit of knowledge and progress.

Famous Aviators and Their Contributions to Aviation History

Throughout the rich tapestry of aviation history, numerous individuals have left an indelible mark on the world of flight. From daring record-setters to pioneers who shattered barriers, this section highlights some of the most notable aviators and their significant contributions to aviation.

Bessie Coleman: Defying All Odds

Bessie Coleman, an African American aviator born in 1892, defied the social norms and overcame racial and gender barriers to become the world's first licensed African American pilot. Denied entrance to aviation schools in the United States due to discrimination, Coleman traveled to France in 1920 to receive her pilot's license from the Fédération Aéronautique Internationale. Upon her return to America, she became a trailblazer for African Americans in aviation, breaking down barriers and inspiring future generations of aviators.

Charles Lindbergh: The Spirit of St. Louis

In 1927, Charles Lindbergh captured the world's imagination when he made the first solo nonstop transatlantic flight from New York to Paris aboard the Spirit of St. Louis. His daring feat showcased the potential of long-distance flight. It cemented his status as an international hero and a symbol of aviation prowess.

Amelia Earhart: The Queen of the Air

Amelia Earhart, a pioneering aviator born in 1897, became the first woman to fly solo across the Atlantic Ocean in 1932. Known for her courage and adventurous spirit, Earhart set multiple aviation records and played a crucial role in promoting women's involvement in aviation. Her mysterious disappearance during an attempted flight around the world in 1937 only deepened her fascination with her extraordinary life and achievements.

Chuck Yeager: Breaking the Sound Barrier

In 1947 U.S. Air Force pilot Chuck Yeager was the first to break the sound barrier, reaching Mach 1 in the Bell X-1 aircraft. His achievement not only pushed the boundaries of what was thought possible but also opened the door to supersonic flight, paving the way for future advancements in aerospace technology.

Yuri Gagarin: The First Human in Space

On April 12, 1961, Yuri Gagarin, a Soviet cosmonaut, made history by becoming the first human to journey into space aboard the Vostok 1 spacecraft. Gagarin's successful orbital flight marked a significant milestone in space exploration, sparking the space race between the United States and the Soviet Union.

Neil Armstrong: One Small Step for Man

In 1969, American astronaut Neil Armstrong etched his name in history when he became the first person to set foot on the Moon during the Apollo 11 mission. His iconic words, "That's one small step for man, one giant leap for mankind," echoed across the globe, symbolizing humanity's triumph in space exploration.

Valentina Tereshkova: The First Woman in Space

In 1963, Valentina Tereshkova, a Soviet cosmonaut, became the first woman to fly to space aboard Vostok 6. Her mission broke gender barriers and demonstrated that women were equally capable of venturing into the cosmos.

Bob Hoover: The Pilot's Pilot

Bob Hoover, an American aviator, was renowned for his extraordinary flying skills and contributions to aviation safety. As a World War II fighter pilot and later a famous air show performer, Hoover's precision flying and mastery of aerobatics earned him the moniker "The Pilot's Pilot."

These aviators, among many others, have left a lasting legacy that continues to inspire and shape the world of aviation. Their courage, determination, and groundbreaking accomplishments have expanded the horizons of human flight and ignited the imaginations of future generations. As their stories intertwine with the history of aviation, these pioneers serve as a reminder that the skies hold endless possibilities for those who dare to dream and reach for the stars.

Innovators in Aircraft Design and Engineering: From Jack Northrop to Alexander Lippisch

The world of aviation has been propelled forward by visionary minds who pushed the boundaries of aircraft design and engineering. This section delves into the lives and achievements of two prominent innovators, Jack Northrop and Alexander Lippisch, who left an indelible mark on the evolution of flight.

Jack Northrop: Shaping the Future of Aircraft

Jack Northrop, an American aviation engineer and founder of the Northrop Corporation, was a trailblazer in aircraft design during the early to mid-20th century. He pioneered flying-wing aircraft configurations, envisioning planes with minimal conventional fuselages and tail structures. His early designs, such as the Northrop N-1M and N-9M, explored the aerodynamic advantages of the flying-wing concept.

Northrop's most significant contribution came with the development of the YB-35 and YB-49 flying-wing bombers, which were ahead of their time. While the YB-35 and YB-49 faced some technical challenges and were eventually phased out, they laid the foundation for the future development of stealth aircraft and advanced flying-wing designs. Northrop's unwavering commitment to his vision set the stage for future innovations in aerospace engineering.

Alexander Lippisch: A Visionary in Supersonic Flight

Alexander Lippisch, a German aeronautical engineer, pioneered studying high-speed flight and delta wing configurations. His work in the 1920s and 1930s on delta-wing gliders, such as Delta I and Delta II, led to valuable insights into the aerodynamics of supersonic flight. These early experiments laid the groundwork for developing delta-winged supersonic aircraft in later years.

Lippisch's most significant contribution came with the Messerschmitt Me 163 Komet, a rocket-powered interceptor designed for high-speed engagements during World War II. The Me 163 became the world's first operational rocket-powered aircraft. It held the distinction of being the fastest aircraft of its time. Lippisch's innovative designs and groundbreaking research on delta wings continue to influence modern high-speed aircraft development.

The legacies of Jack Northrop and Alexander Lippisch endure in the continued advancements of aviation technology. Their revolutionary ideas and bold experiments have inspired generations of aerospace engineers to strive for innovation and excellence in aircraft design. As aviation continues to soar to new heights, the contributions of these innovators serve as a testament to the boundless possibilities of human ingenuity in shaping the skies above.

Unsung Heroes and Innovators Shaping the Future of Aviation

Beyond the well-known pioneers of aviation, countless unsung heroes and innovators have played pivotal roles in shaping aviation history. This section pays tribute to remarkable individuals whose contributions have often gone unnoticed. Yet, their innovations continue to influence the future of flight.

Jerrie Cobb: Breaking Barriers in Aerospace

Jerrie Cobb, an American aviator, was a trailblazer in the aerospace field and a staunch advocate for women in aviation. In the early 1960s, she underwent rigorous testing as part of the "Mercury 13" program, a group of highly qualified women pilots who underwent astronaut training in preparation for space missions. Although the program was ultimately canceled by NASA, Cobb's determination and dedication paved the way for future female astronauts.

Hélène Boucher: A French Aviation Pioneer

Hélène Boucher, a French aviator, captured the world's imagination with her incredible piloting skills and daring spirit during the 1930s. She set numerous speed records, including the women's world speed record. She was a symbol of courage and achievement in aviation. Tragically, her life was cut short at 26 in a plane crash. Still, her legacy endures as an inspiration for aspiring aviators.

Theodore von Kármán: Advancing Aeronautics and Astronautics

Theodore von Kármán, a Hungarian-American aerospace engineer, was a driving force behind many significant advancements in aeronautics and astronautics. He founded the Jet Propulsion Laboratory (JPL) and was crucial in developing supersonic and hypersonic flight. Von Kármán's work laid the foundation for future space exploration. It solidified his place as one of the foremost aerospace engineers of the 20th century.

Hedy Lamarr: The Actress and Inventor

A Hollywood actress, Hedy Lamarr may be best known for her work on the silver screen. Still, she was also an inventor whose contributions significantly impacted aviation. During World War II, Lamarr co-developed a frequency-hopping spread spectrum technology to prevent enemy jamming of torpedoes. Although initially overlooked, her invention became a crucial precursor to modern wireless communication technologies.

Max Munk: The Aerodynamics Visionary

An Austrian-American engineer, Max Munk, made pioneering contributions to aerodynamics during the early 20th century. He conducted extensive research on airfoil designs and airflow patterns, leading to the development of more efficient wing profiles. Munk's work laid the groundwork for improved aircraft performance and fuel efficiency, contributing to advancing aviation technology.

These unsung heroes, among many others, have left an indelible mark on the world of aviation. Their resilience, creativity, and passion for flight have enriched the aerospace field and continue to inspire future aviators and innovators. As we celebrate the achievements of these remarkable individuals, we recognize that the future of aviation rests on the collective efforts of those who dare to dream and push the boundaries of human exploration.

The Beauty of Flight: Aesthetics and Airshows

The Artistic Aspect of Aircraft Design: Form and Function

B eyond practical purposes, airplanes possess a captivating aesthetic quality that blends form with function. This uncovers the artistic aspect of aircraft design, exploring how engineers and designers harmonize aesthetics with engineering principles to create masterpieces of flight.

Form Follows Function: The Marriage of Design and Purpose

Throughout aviation history, engineers and designers have adhered to the "form follows function." This design philosophy emphasizes that an aircraft's shape and appearance are primarily driven by its intended purpose and performance requirements. From the streamlined curves of supersonic jets to the elegant simplicity of vintage biplanes, every aspect of an aircraft's design serves a specific function: reducing drag, enhancing stability, or improving maneuverability.

The Allure of Classic Designs: Vintage Aircraft Restoration

Preserving the beauty and historical significance of vintage aircraft is a labor of love for aviation enthusiasts. This section highlights the meticulous process of restoring and maintaining classic airplanes, from World War II fighters to iconic passenger airliners. The dedication of skilled artisans and volunteers ensures that these timeless aircraft continue to grace the skies, providing a nostalgic glimpse into aviation's golden age.

Airshows: A Symphony of Flight and Spectacle

Airshows are breathtaking displays of skill and artistry that celebrate the wonder of flight. This section offers a behind-the-scenes look at the preparation and execution of these captivating events, where aerobatic teams and solo performers showcase the full potential of their aircraft. From gravity-defying maneuvers to perfectly choreographed formations, airshows are a testament to the extraordinary capabilities of modern aircraft and the skill of their pilots.

Livery and Aircraft Liveries: The Canvas of Identity

In the vast world of aviation, aircraft liveries go beyond mere branding; they are the vibrant and dynamic canvases that breathe life into the identity of airlines and aviation organizations. These iconic designs, crafted with meticulous care, represent the essence of an airline's character, history, and values. The creative process involves a delicate balance between aesthetics and functionality, selecting colors, themes, and design elements that resonate with the airline's brand identity.

From bold and striking hues to cultural symbols and iconic landmarks, these liveries become soaring emblems visible from afar, connecting travelers to the airlines they patronize and leaving a lasting impression on aviation enthusiasts worldwide. As the aircraft traverse the skies, these flying works of art spark wonder and forge a connection that unites humanity through the shared love of flight.

The Evolution of Design Trends: From Classic to Futuristic

The evolution of design trends has been a captivating journey through time, showcasing the remarkable metamorphosis of aircraft aesthetics from classic to futuristic. In the archives of aviation history, we find a treasure trove of iconic classic aircraft that graced the skies with their timeless elegance and enduring beauty. These vintage marvels, with their distinct silhouettes and graceful lines, evoke a sense of nostalgia and admiration for the pioneers who first conquered the heavens. As technology progressed, the baton of the design was passed to the present, where contemporary aircraft don sophisticated liveries and modern aerodynamic profiles, reflecting the spirit of our times. Bold and imaginative liveries adorn commercial jets, celebrating diverse cultures and capturing the imagination of travelers worldwide. Yet, the journey into the future of aviation design knows no bounds.

With every stride in aerodynamics, materials science, and cutting-edge technologies, visionary concepts emerge, teasing us with a glimpse of what lies ahead. Futuristic aircraft designs break free from conventional norms, presenting sleek and streamlined forms that challenge our perceptions of what flight could be. The evolution of design trends continues to be an awe-inspiring symphony, where the past echoes in harmony with the future, reminding us that the beauty of aviation lies not only in engineering triumphs but also in the ever-evolving artistry of flight.

The Allure of Airshows and Aerobatic Performances

Airshows and aerobatic performances are exhilarating displays of skill, precision, and daring that captivate audiences world-wide. This section explores the allure of these events, delving into the heart-pounding excitement and sheer artistry that makes them a cherished tradition in aviation.

A Symphony of Precision: The Art of Aerobatics

Aerobatic performances are a testament to the extraordinary abilities of pilots and aircraft. This section showcases the incredible skill and training required to perform gravity-defying maneuvers with split-second precision. From loop-the-loops and barrel rolls to knife-edge flights, aerobatic pilots push the limits of human and machine, pushing themselves to the edge of the envelope in a mesmerizing display of mastery over flight.

The Thrill of Formation Flying

The thrill of formation flying ignites the skies with electrifying energy, captivating aviation enthusiasts and spectators alike. This exhilarating spectacle brings to life the remarkable prowess of pilots, showcasing their exceptional skills and unwavering camaraderie. As a squadron of aircraft takes to the heavens, they become a symphony of precision and grace, moving in perfect harmony. The heart-stopping maneuvers and tight formations achieved with meticulous coordination and flawless communication leave spectators breathless with wonder and amazement. The sense of unity among the pilots is palpable, their trust and reliance on one another forming an unbreakable bond that propels them to reach new heights of mastery. The spectacle of formation flying epitomizes the audacious spirit of aviation, where the pursuit of excellence meets the sheer thrill of pushing the boundaries of what is possible in the sky.

Airshow Stunts

Pushing boundaries and igniting imaginations, airshows transcend mere entertainment, becoming magnificent platforms for aerial artistry and technological prowess. This section unravels the realm of modern fighter jets and high-performance aircraft as they take center stage in a symphony of daring acrobatics and breathtaking stunts. The skies become a canvas for audacious displays as these cutting-edge marvels execute high-speed passes that blur the line between machine and lightning and dramatic vertical climbs that defy the very laws of gravity. Each maneuver becomes a daring dance of engineering brilliance and unwavering courage, pushing the boundaries of what is conceivable in flight. As the thunderous roar of engines resonates through the air, audiences find themselves spellbound, their hearts racing with excitement and their imaginations ignited with wonder. The spectacle of airshows becomes a captivating ode to human ingenuity, a testament to the indomitable spirit that urges us to reach for the skies and embrace the limitless possibilities of aviation.

The Showmanship of Aerobatic Performers

Aerobatic pilots transcend the realm of ordinary aviators; they emerge as captivating performers, their every maneuver a mesmerizing act that both entertains and inspires. Here we discuss the world of these skilled aviators, where showmanship and charisma take center stage. They weave a narrative that draws the audience into their spectacle with every twist, turn, and loop. It is not merely a display of flying prowess; it is a symphony of storytelling where the pilots become masterful narrators, guiding spectators through the ethereal realm of aviation with their words and flight. Through passionate communication, they open a window into their love for the skies, sharing anecdotes of their soaring experiences that captivate the imagination and awaken a sense of wonder. As they fly, a magical connection transcends the boundaries between the cockpit and the mesmerized crowd below. In the thunderous symphony of engines and the graceful dance of flight, these aviators paint a portrait of boundless passion and a soaring spirit that resonates deeply with all who witness their aerial artistry.

The Global Stage: International Airshows and Competitions

In the captivating world of aviation, international airshows and competitions serve as the global stage, uniting enthusiasts and aviation fans from all corners of the globe. These celebrated events showcase the prowess of skilled pilots who converge from diverse nations, dazzling audiences with daring aerobatic displays that push the boundaries of flight. The skies become an ethereal canvas where art and engineering intertwine as sleek aircraft execute precision maneuvers with grace and precision. Spectators are entranced by the symphony of soaring wings and thundering engines as the love for flight and the spirit of innovation unite on this extraordinary stage. From heart-stopping stunts to breathtaking formations, these airshows celebrate the boundless possibilities of aviation and inspire a profound appreciation for the marvels of flight. As a testament to the enthralling allure of airplanes, this global showcase brings together a community of dreamers and pioneers, all driven by the enduring fascination with the wonders of the sky.

Historic Airshows and the Evolution of Aviation Exhibitions

The history of aviation exhibitions and airshows dates back to the early 20th century, marking significant milestones in aviation development and capturing people's imaginations worldwide.

The Birth of Flight Demonstrations

As aviation pioneers took to the skies for the first time, they recognized the importance of showcasing their achievements to a broader audience. Early flight demonstrations, often held at fairs and exhibitions, gave spectators a glimpse of the seemingly impossible dream of human flight becoming a reality. These events showcased rudimentary aircraft, captivating onlookers with novelty and daring feats.

Air Races: Pushing the Limits of Speed and Endurance

In the early 20th century, air races became a prominent feature of aviation exhibitions. Pilots competed to set records for speed and endurance, pushing their aircraft's and themselves' limits. These races demonstrated progress in aviation technology and fueled the public's fascination with the brave aviators who dared to fly faster and farther.

The Golden Age of Airshows

The 1920s and 1930s witnessed the emergence of the "Golden Age" of airshows, characterized by barnstorming and daredevil aerobatics. Barnstormers, thrill-seeking aviators, traveled from town to town, putting on breathtaking aerial displays that included loops, spins, and death-defying stunts. These performances were instrumental in popularizing aviation and inspiring the next generation of pilots.

Airshows during World War II

World War II brought a shift like airshows, as military aircraft were showcased for propaganda and recruitment. Airshows became opportunities for countries to demonstrate their military prowess and rally public support for the war effort. Fighter planes engaged in simulated dogfights, and bomber formations showcased the might of airpower.

Post-War Airshows: The Age of Jet Aviation

After World War II, the advent of jet aviation revolutionized airshows, ushering in a new era of speed and agility. Jet fighters, such as the legendary North American F-86 Sabre and the Soviet

MiG-15, thrilled audiences with their supersonic capabilities. Airshows became platforms for countries to showcase technological advancements and compete for aerospace dominance.

Modern Airshows: Celebrating Innovation and Unity

Today, airshows continue to captivate audiences worldwide, featuring cutting-edge aircraft and aerial performances that push the boundaries of flight. Modern airshows emphasize the spectacle of aerobatics and the celebration of innovation and international cooperation. These events testify to the shared passion for aviation and the enduring spirit of exploration.

Modern Airshows: Showcasing Cutting-Edge Technology and Breathtaking Maneuvers

In the 21st century, modern airshows have evolved into spectacular events that showcase the pinnacle of aviation technology and push the boundaries of aerial performance. With an emphasis on innovation, precision, and entertainment, these airshows continue to captivate audiences with breathtaking maneuvers and awe-inspiring displays.

Technological Marvels in the Sky

Modern airshows feature an array of technologically advanced aircraft that represent the cutting edge of aviation. Each aircraft on display, from state-of-the-art fighter jets to high-performance aerobatic planes, demonstrates the incredible progress made in aerospace engineering. The integration of advanced avionics, lightweight materials, and robust engines enables these aircraft to achieve feats that were once considered impossible.

Thrilling Aerobatic Performances

Aerobatic teams and solo pilots take center stage at modern airshows, wowing the crowds with their daring and precise maneuvers. These skilled aviators execute intricate aerial ballets featuring loops, rolls, spins, and gravity-defying stunts. The seamless coordination and split-second timing required in these performances showcases the extraordinary skill and training these pilots possess.

Jet-Powered Aerobatics

The introduction of jet-powered aerobatic aircraft has taken air-shows to new heights. Jet teams, like the renowned Blue Angels and Thunderbirds, demonstrate the exceptional capabilities of modern fighter jets with their high-speed passes and formation flying. The thunderous roar of jet engines reverberates through the air, leaving audiences in awe of the power and agility of these incredible machines.

Drone Displays: A Futuristic Spectacle

In recent years, drone displays have emerged as a futuristic and mesmerizing addition to airshows. Choreographed formations of synchronized drones create stunning visual spectacles, form-ing intricate patterns and dynamic shapes in the sky. These drone performances demonstrate the versatility of crewless aerial vehicles and their potential applications in various industries.

Interactive Airshow Experiences

Modern airshows go beyond aerial displays, offering interactive experiences for spectators on the ground. Aviation enthusiasts can explore static aircraft displays, getting up close to some of the most advanced flying machines in the world. Additionally, aviation technology exhibitions and educational booths provide insights into the science and engineering behind flight.

Promoting Safety and Responsible Flying

Amid the excitement and thrill of airshows, safety remains a top priority. Airshow organizers work closely with aviation authorities to ensure strict safety protocols are followed. These events also serve as opportunities to promote responsible flying and raise awareness about aviation safety among the public.

As modern airshows continue to evolve, they reaffirm the fascination with flight and the passion of those who dedicate their lives to aviation. From the exhilarating performances in the sky to the celebration of innovation and human achievement, these events inspire wonder and appreciation for the art and science of aviation. Through the lens of modern airshows, the world witnesses the harmony of human skill and technological prowess, united in the pursuit of soaring above the horizon.

The Human Connection to Flight: How Airshows Inspire and Captivate Audiences

Airshows holds a unique place in people's hearts worldwide, transcending cultural boundaries and captivating audiences of all ages. Beyond the displays of aviation technology and skill, airshows evoke a profound sense of wonder, inspiration, and nostalgia. They serve as a platform for celebrating the human connection to flight and the indomitable spirit of exploration.

An Expression of Human Ingenuity

From the earliest attempts at flight to the marvels of modern aviation, airshows are a testament to human ingenuity and perseverance. The desire to conquer the skies has driven inventors, aviators, and engineers to push the limits of what is possible. Airshows celebrate flight milestones, paying homage to the pioneers who dared to dream and soar above the horizon.

Inspiring the Next Generation

Airshows provide a thrilling and tangible flight experience for spectators, particularly for young minds eager to explore the world's wonders. The sight of powerful aircraft executing gravity-defying maneuvers can ignite a spark of curiosity and ambition in the hearts of future pilots, engineers, and innovators. For many children, airshows become a defining moment that plants the seed of passion for aviation.

Fostering a Sense of Community

Airshows bring people together in celebration of a shared passion for flight. Families, aviation enthusiasts, and curious onlookers gather to witness the majesty of aircraft dancing in the sky. The camaraderie and excitement foster a sense of community among attendees, fostering new friendships and connections forged through a mutual love for aviation.

A Showcase of National Pride

For many nations, airshows represent a source of pride, showcasing their technological prowess and military capabilities. National aerobatic teams and demonstration flights symbolize the skill and dedication of their respective armed forces. These displays demonstrate the might of nations and serve as a platform for fostering international friendships and cooperation.

Celebrating Human Achievement

Airshows celebrate the human potential for achievement and excellence. They honor the dedication and training of pilots and ground crews who work tirelessly to ensure the safety and success of each performance. The courage and skill displayed by aerobatic pilots exemplify the heights that human determination can reach, inspiring for overcoming challenges in all aspects of life.

A Temporary Escape from Reality

For spectators, airshows provide a temporary escape from the complexities of daily life. The captivating performances and the thrill of witnessing daring feats offer a momentary respite, allowing attendees to immerse themselves in the magic of flight. The sky becomes a canvas upon which dreams take flight, igniting a sense of wonder and adventure.

Airshows are much more than exhibitions of aviation prowess; they celebrate the human spirit. Through these dynamic and captivating events, we are reminded of the remarkable progress of aviation, the enduring nature of exploration, and the capacity of humanity to reach new heights. As we gather to witness the majesty of flight, airshows become a testament to the eternal desire to soar above the horizon and embrace the boundless possibilities that lie beyond.

Conclusion

Reflecting on the Wonder of Flight and Its Impact on Humanity

As we conclude this journey through aviation, we find ourselves in awe of the wonder of flight and its profound impact on humanity. From the audacious dreams of the Wright brothers to the cutting-edge technology of modern spaceplanes, aviation has shaped our world in once unimaginable ways. It has transcended borders, connected cultures, and inspired generations to reach for the skies.

Recapitulation of Remarkable Airplane Facts and Discoveries

Throughout this book, we have explored the remarkable facts and discoveries that have shaped the history of aviation. We delved into the evolution of airplane materials, the significance of different airframe configurations, and the crucial role of flight controls in maneuvering aircraft. We examined the innovations in aviation safety, flight's environmental impact, and space exploration's boundless possibilities. Along the way, we celebrated the pioneers, aviators, and innovators who have left an indelible mark on the world of flight.

Envisioning the Future of Aviation and Its Potential for

Innovation and Sustainability

As we look to the future, the horizon of aviation stretches far beyond our imagination. The boundless potential for innovation and sustainability promises greener skies, advanced space exploration, and safer skies for all. The collaborative efforts of the aviation industry, governments, and passionate individuals continue to push the boundaries of what is possible, inspiring us to believe that the best is yet to come.

In the ever-changing world of aviation, one thing remains constant: the human spirit's unyielding desire to explore and conquer the skies. From the early dreams of flight to the daring space missions of the future, aviation will forever be a symbol of human ingenuity, determination, and unity.

Soaring Beyond the Horizon has been a celebration of the marvels of flight and a tribute to the individuals who have made it possible. As we close this chapter, let us carry with us the profound understanding that the sky is not the limit—it is a gateway to uncharted territories and a reminder of the boundless potential within each of us.

As we bid farewell to these pages, may our hearts be filled with the wonder of flight, and may our dreams take flight as we continue to reach new heights, embracing the skies with unwavering curiosity and courage. The aviation journey is eternal, and together, we shall soar beyond the horizon, forever chasing the sunsets and the stars.

Call to Action

Thank you for embarking on this exhilarating journey through aviation in "Soaring Beyond the Horizon: Unveiling Extraordinary Airplane Facts and Discoveries." Your support and curiosity have allowed us to explore the wonders of flight and the pioneering individuals who have shaped its course.

If you enjoyed the book and found it as captivating as we did while writing it, we would be incredibly grateful if you could leave a review on Amazon. Your feedback and thoughts will inspire us to continue sharing fascinating aviation stories and help other readers discover the joy of exploring the skies through this book.

Your review will serve as a testament to the remarkable world of aviation and the incredible community of readers who share in its wonder. By leaving a review, you become an essential part of our flight crew, helping to chart the course for future aviation and space exploration adventures.

We sincerely appreciate your time and support in leaving a review. Let's inspire others to soar beyond the horizon and embrace the limitless possibilities of flight.

Resources

Aerospace Industries Association (AIA). (https://www.aia-aero space.org/)

Airbus. (https://www.airbus.com/)

Anderson, J. D. (2019). Introduction to Flight (8th ed.). McGraw-Hill Education.

Aviation Week Network. (https://aviationweek.com/)

Boeing. (https://www.boeing.com/)

Clancy, L. J. (2019). Aerodynamics. John Wiley & Sons.

Crane, D. (2016). The World Encyclopedia of Fighters & Bombers: An Illustrated History of the World's Greatest Military Aircraft. Lorenz Books.

Federal Aviation Administration (FAA). (https://www.faa.gov/)

FlightGlobal. (https://www.flightglobal.com/)

Hallion, R. P. (2016). Taking Flight: Inventing the Aerial Age, from Antiquity Through the First World War. Oxford University

Press.

International Civil Aviation Organization (ICAO). (https://www.icao.int/)

Johnson, R. A. (2017). Aircraft Structures for Engineering Students (6th ed.). Butterworth-Heinemann.

National Aeronautics and Space Administration (NASA). (https://www.nasa.gov/)

National Geographic: Air and Space. (https://www.nationalgeographic.com/air-and-space-magazine/)

Royal Aeronautical Society. (https://www.aerosociety.com/)

Smithsonian National Air and Space Museum. (https://airandspace.si.edu/)

Society of Experimental Test Pilots (SETP). (https://www.setp.org/)

Space.com. (https://www.space.com/)

The Royal Air Force Museum. (https://www.rafmuseum.org.uk/)

AIAA Aerospace Research Central. (https://arc.aiaa.org/)